'Brad Marshall may well ha[...] problematic internet use cases than anyone else in the [...]. His timely and accessible book is packed with useful ideas and tips, and numerous vividly drawn case vignettes based on clinical experience. It is informative, down-to-earth, often very funny and, most importantly, contains lots of practical suggestions for the time-poor, but device-rich, modern family struggling to achieve a healthy digital balance.

Every concerned parent should get a copy. Then they should get their teenager to read it also.'

– Dr Philip GE Tam
Child and Adolescent Psychiatrist

'This easy-to-read, step-by-step guide will be invaluable to parents trying to manage digital device use within their families because the methods Brad Marshall provides are based on thousands of hours of successful clinical treatment. Importantly, Brad doesn't sidestep the thorny issues around children and teens with addictive levels of screen use. He gives concrete advice on how to manage kids who become difficult or even violent when asked to reduce screen use, how to respond to common screen-use justifications, and how to set up a workable plan for digital device use that takes into account key developmental needs.'

– Dr Wayne Warburton PhD
Associate Professor of Developmental Psychology,
Macquarie University

'*The Tech Diet for Your Child & Teen* is not simply a timely and practical book – it is a *necessary* book. Readers will be the beneficiaries of the author's vast experience treating countless young people and families affected by technology. The numerous tips will not only help parents feel empowered but will also, in all likelihood, work!'

– Professor Garry Walter AM
Child, Adolescent and Family Psychiatrist

HarperCollins*Publishers*

First published in Australia in 2019
by HarperCollins*Publishers* Australia Pty Limited
ABN 36 009 913 517
harpercollins.com.au

HarperCollins*Publishers*

Level 13, 201 Elizabeth Street, Sydney, NSW 2000, Australia
Unit D1, 63 Apollo Drive, Rosedale, Auckland 0632, New Zealand
A 53, Sector 57, Noida, UP, India
1 London Bridge Street, London, SE1 9GF, United Kingdom
Bay Adelaide Centre, East Tower, 22 Adelaide Street West, 41st Floor,
     Toronto, Ontario, M5H 4E3, Canada
195 Broadway, New York, NY 10007

A catalogue record for this book is available from the National Library of Australia

ISBN: 978 1 4607 5801 4 (paperback)
ISBN: 978 1 4607 1176 7 (ebook : epub)

Cover design by Hazel Lam, HarperCollins Design Studio
Cover image by shutterstock.com
Internal design by Renée Bahr @Post Pre-press
Author portrait by Ryan Stuart Photography
Printed and bound in Australia by McPherson's Printing Group

The papers used by HarperCollins in the manufacture of this book are a natural, recyclable product made from wood grown in sustainable plantation forests. The fibre source and manufacturing processes meet recognised international environmental standards, and carry certification.

The
Tech
Diet for your
Child & Teen

Brad Marshall

HarperCollinsPublishers
Australia

To my wife and daughter, who always support me
when new projects and adventures seek me out.
I want that you are always happy.

Contents

Contents

INTRODUCTION

Before we begin, let's set the record straight.

My Unplugged Steps should not be taken literally.

I'm not suggesting you should pack your kids in the car and go off-grid like there's a zombie apocalypse upon us. For anyone scoffing, that's been suggested as a solution by parents on more than one occasion in my office.

At the same time, we can't just put our hands up, let our kids have free rein and hope their underdeveloped brains will be able to resist the allure of screens.

The word 'balance' is thrown around a lot when discussing this topic.

> **This book provides tangible measures of balance for children and teenagers, and real-world strategies to bring their Tech Diet back to a good place.**

Terminology ...

I use the terms 'children', 'kids' and 'teenagers' interchangeably at times. Don't get too bogged down in age brackets. **My approach is relevant to help kids of any age – anyone currently having problems using technology – and to set up a solid foundation before things get too out of hand for younger kids, who may not yet have reached the slippery slope.**

If you're an adult reading this book to reflect on your own Tech Diet, then welcome. If you're an adult reading this so you can make notes on all the points you disagree with – don't waste your time. As an adult, you're free to make your own decisions and live your life. You do you.

In psychology, we sometimes like to use fancy words that make us sound important. **In this book, I'll provide a commonsense, no bullsh*t opinion on how to implement a Tech Diet for your child.**

If at any time you're pulling out your phone to look up a definition on the internet, then I've failed.

What am I signing up for?

I'm not pushing a magical cure.
This will be hard work.

If you're just dipping your toe in the water, this is a good starting point.

This book will take you through a journey of three stages:

1 **I'll explain the research and literature in a way that won't put you to sleep.**
I won't go too deep. I've refined this from being invited to speak at countless parent talks where I get instant feedback, creating a plan that has the right amount and type of research that parents can take in on this topic. Many of my parent talks start at local schools at 6 pm or 7 pm – prime time for work-weary parents to have a quick kip while I speak. I think I've found the point where I no longer get napping parents in my talks. The research is a necessary evil. I'll give it to you straight. **If you dismiss, don't understand or skip this part, you're far less likely to succeed with implementing the practical strategies.**

2 **I'll address the burning question: when should parents panic?**

In other words, I'll go into detail about the warning signs that your child or teenager is on the path to Internet or Screen Addiction, and a way to grasp just how far down that path you are. This will help you weigh up how hard you want to go in implementing the Tech Diet.

3 **We'll talk turkey.**

If you've read other books or interviews with experts, they typically suggest you 'write up a plan or contract' with your child to encourage a healthy balance. In my experience, these are light on detail or you get a general proforma. Some books include a few pages on this area and that's it – an afterthought.

That should work, right? No. **I've negotiated so many tech plans in my clinic I've lost count.**

There are some core elements that are the basis of every good Tech Diet. I call them the Unplugged Steps. Followed by a whole host of other variables, factors, curve balls and troubleshooting that need to be considered.

With this book, I provide you with a comprehensive guide to a realistic Tech Diet.

My story

I'm not an accomplished author. Heck, I didn't even do very well in HSC English.

I'm not an academic. While I'm largely across the research in my field, I certainly don't claim to be an expert in the nuances of neuropsychology and statistical analysis that litter most journal articles.

I'm a clinician. A psychologist who helps children, teenagers and families facing the reality of Gaming Disorder.

I wrote this book because I feel I have something to offer parents at home.

There are other great books on this topic. Some of them focus heavily on the research and statistics with important, but laborious, detail of the studies. Others focus on younger children and skip over the trickiest teenage years. While I value and respect these opinions, overall, there aren't many that come from the perspective of a clinician – **someone who actually treats children and teenagers in a clinic, day in, day out.**

I grew up in Sydney's inner west during the late 1980s and early 1990s. My introduction to gaming and the internet came care of dial-up modems, where the world was limitless so long as your older brother didn't pick up the landline phone in the process.

My vice? ICQ – the original social media messenger, for you millennials out there – and Alex Kidd on Sega Master System. As a teenager, I played endless hours of Doom on the family computer and Mario Kart and GoldenEye 007 on Nintendo 64 with a group of mates huddled around the four-player split screen TV, in between bike rides and destroying the family swimming pool.

Fast-forward two decades and most parents can tell you things have changed. Not only do I no longer need a landline phone, but **gaming is far more sophisticated and the much-maligned Australian internet connection allows children and teenagers access to a social world without ever leaving their bedroom.**

Being a male psychologist in the field, I receive more referrals for boys than I do girls. Not something I planned … I suppose parents believe their sons will connect better with a male? I don't even feel that's necessarily true, but that's what happens in practice in my clinic.

Personally, I now sport many hats: psychologist, business owner, mate, husband, somewhat unskilled home handyman and, most challenging of all, parent.

'You're it.'

Almost 10 years ago, I sat in a team meeting at a public hospital in Sydney while my colleagues discussed a referral for a young boy engrossed in gaming. I can recall him logging on to a Harry Potter virtual world simulator of sorts, where each person had a character who mirrored the hit series and roles. The boy explained to me he had taken on a very important teaching role at Hogwarts in which other people from around the world would attend his class and play out the story in this virtual school of magic.

His online world had encapsulated him to the point of paralysis. He was refusing to attend school, had lost contact with his real-world friends, and his general mental health was in total free-fall.

The discussion turned to who was going to see this boy. A much more senior colleague looked at me and said, **'Brad, you're it.'**

I shook my head and replied, 'What do you mean "I'm it"? I don't know anything about gaming addiction.'

My colleague rebutted, 'You play video games, right? So you know more than anyone else here. You're it.'

So I was it.

Little did I know that those words would prepare me
for an epidemic, of sorts, that would lead to a dedicated
clinic at Northshore Kidspace for children and teenagers
suffering Internet and Screen Addiction.

The front line

It's fair to say the field of Internet Addiction is scrambling.
We can't even agree on a universal term, let alone a set of
diagnostic criteria.

Do we call it Problematic Use?
Internet Addiction?
Screen Addiction?
Gaming Disorder?
Or any number of other variations?

While many colleagues gallantly work to contribute to the
field of research, I describe myself more as the front line.

> **I see the children and families whose
> lives are often torn apart by technology.
> I'm less concerned about the semantics
> of what to call the problem and more
> interested in helping parents and
> families reclaim their children.**

Taking a smartphone from an adult is challenging.

Taking a smartphone from a teenager can be explosive.

How did we get to this point?

CHAPTER 1

GENERATION SMARTPHONE

Smartphone: never leave home without it

Smartphones have found a way to intertwine themselves with our very existence. That's not necessarily a negative thing. And it's in no way intended to come across as judgemental. I'm one of the millions of Australians who confess to taking their smartphone to the toilet. Come on, you trying to tell me you still read magazines in there?!

Smartphones have enriched our lives in many ways, and **I, for one, don't advocate the 'blow up the smartphones' nuclear option some may assume is going to follow from a book claiming to be Unplugged.**

There's been a recent media uproar around developing rules for phone use in schools. This is such an important debate and discussion for our community to have. Many years ago, I saw an influx of teenagers with access to smartphones at school. This was around the same time that large sections of parents demanded schools embrace technology for educational purposes. It was done in haste, and largely without considering the possible downsides.

One group of American researchers found rates of mental health symptoms such as depression increased among teenagers between 2010 and 2015.[1] The authors reported that **teenagers with higher rates of social media use had higher rates of mental health issues than those who spent more time in real-world social activities.**

There is a school of thought that this rise is closely correlated with smartphone ownership becoming more mainstream from 2010.

Personally, I think it does pass the commonsense test.

I'm simply saying we need to be aware of the relationship we have with our smartphones and, most importantly, the possible negatives they can have on our children and teenagers.

The easier it is for your kids to access social media and messaging services via their smartphones, the less time they spend in the real world.

Why did mindfulness go mainstream?

If you're not aware of mindfulness, the simplest way I can explain it is to do an activity that requires you to continue to focus on what you're doing, and every time you get distracted, you bring yourself back to the original activity.

Remember a few years back there was this huge push for mindfulness and the benefits it has on your mental health? Corporate Australia lapped up this concept. And to be fair, there is a substantial body of research to back up the positive benefits of mindfulness. This led to an avalanche of everything from businesses offering mindfulness sessions for their staff, to mindfulness classes for primary school-aged kids, and my personal favourite: the adult colouring book phenomenon you will find in every good bookstore, no doubt outselling this book!

Before the pro-mindfulness brigade crucifies me, **I want to be clear that I do think it's an amazing strategy for managing stress and anxiety.**

However, I do wonder if the mindfulness craze was born out of necessity to combat our lost skills since smartphones took over.

Using technology to solve boredom

If you're at a restaurant and your child is bored and restless because the food is taking a while, many moons ago they would be forced to do any number of real-world activities like colouring, reading or playing with other kids.

All these activities have an element of mindfulness to them. We didn't call it that, but being connected to the world was one of the unintended benefits.

Now, don't cringe or start cursing if you're one of these parents, but it's easy to give our kids a smartphone or tablet in this situation. Self-confessed, I've done it before in a moment of weakness when I was sick, tired and solo parenting (my wife has far more patience than I do).

Research gaps

I often tell parents that research in this field is woefully behind the technology.

We have some studies pointing to the potential impact smartphones have on our children's mental health, but it's such a broad topic we don't know the specifics.

Q Is it just social media that does this?

Q Is it any screen?

Q Is there a perfect number of hours that daily use should be limited to?

I don't have all the answers.

All I can do is offer my experience and try to connect the dots with you.

Even the most tech-savvy parents struggle to understand the allure of modern-day gaming.

I'll explain why it's more attractive than your Nintendo 64 childhood addiction.

CHAPTER 2

THE PSYCH SCIENCE OF GAMING

What's your gaming IQ?

If you happen to be a parent gamer (a parent who enthusiastically enjoys gaming as their own downtime) or you feel you have a good grasp of the basics, **some of this might be familiar, but please don't ignore this section. This is important groundwork.**

If you don't know the general difference between types of games, you can't understand the mechanics. **If you don't understand the mechanics, you'll struggle to troubleshoot when your child's Tech Diet goes off the rails.**

Traditionally, there are a million categories of games: massive multiplayer online (MMO), simulations, sports, adventure, puzzle, action, education, first-person shooter, and the list goes on. But I don't feel these are even relevant categories anymore. You see, game developers have made amazing advances in the last 5 to 10 years, to the point where they've made mega-games that cover many of those categories all in one.

My explanation that follows is designed to be at a level that parents can digest and, no doubt, a true gamer will feel I'm butchering it. I make no apologies.

The three main types of games:

1. Multiplayer online games

In this category, I place any game played online that allows you to play other people. I don't care if those people are your teenager's best mate from school or a bloke from Uzbekistan – it's all the same to me. This might include sport games, combat, shooting games or strategy games.

Some of these games have an option to play against the computer (offline), but most are solely geared to have multiple players or teams duking it out on a server – technical term for an arena that connects all the players.

Traditionally, these types of games have been limited by technology. For example, perhaps the internet speed wasn't quick enough to support them on a mass scale or the game was made for a single console. **These days, games are built to be played across consoles and on many different devices.**

Okay, so I went a tiny bit down the technobabble path just then. Let me shoot straight with an example.

Ten years ago, you bought a game – it was likely one category (for example, sport) – and you played that game on one device. You couldn't link in with friends or strangers. You all needed the same device to play that game.

Today, it's very different.

2. Offline games

Yes, they do still exist. But they're holding on for dear life in today's world.

If you have younger children, they may still be content to play strategy, building or quasi 'educational' (and I use that term loosely) games that are purely offline.

The major distinction is that these games are not played on a server; they're played solely against the computer.

3. Applications, or apps

I think (I hope) you know what apps are. Some of these would be classified in the previous two categories; it just depends on how sophisticated the app is.

In fact, **this category is becoming less relevant.** As smartphones and tablets improve their speed, storage and capacity, they allow the first two categories to move in.

Games leave players feeling they have to come back for more

Here comes the fun part.

I think in the 1980s and 1990s, we all just wrote gaming off as a bit of fun and a laugh.

I put it to you that **the gaming industry is deliberate about the tactics they deploy in games to encourage players.**

That's not a criticism. It's no different from any other company ensuring they make a product that people will enjoy and want to buy.

Here's some of the science, common to many games, that developers use to keep us wanting more and more.

PSYCH SCIENCE #1:

Four player types

Richard Bartle wrote a paper in 1996 (yes, that's over 20 years ago!) where he first defined the Bartle Taxonomy of Player Types.

Essentially, he described what motivates a player to engage with a video game.
It goes a little something like this:

1 Achievers
Those motivated to get through the levels of the game and achieve the pre-set goals in order to gain status.

2 Explorers
Those keen to explore and discover the world created in the game.

3 Socialisers
Those motivated by the friends they make in the game and having a laugh with mates.

4 Killers
Those focused on killing other players, their personal rank and winning the game.

If you're playing along at home, you might be able to see where you landed on the Bartle Taxonomy back in the times when life was simple and you had hours every day to game.

I've already made my confession. For me, it was GoldenEye 007 and Mario Kart. They both had single-player options to play against the computer, but I wasn't interested in that in the slightest.

I played the multiplayer split screen, which allowed four players at a time to battle it out. I was purely a *Socialiser* on the Bartle Taxonomy. I played as a way to socialise with my mates and had little interest in playing against the computer.

Can't understand why I went into a profession that involves talking for a living …

I put it to you that successful modern games have been designed to tick all these categories.

If you sit down with your teenager and ask about how their game works, I'm sure you'll see examples of all four types. There's something for everyone.

PSYCH SCIENCE #2:

Flow

Hands up if you've ever had a conversation with your child or teenager that goes something like this:

You: 'Hey, that's enough. It's time for dinner.'

Teen: ....

You: 'Did you hear me? Dinner. Now!'

Teen: 'Ohhh yeah, just finishing this game now.'

Twenty minutes later you're sitting around an empty table with your husband checking the latest football results on his phone … Sorry, I think we slipped back to my house, but you get the point. You march back into your teenager's room to find **he's started a new game and is claiming your conversation never took place.**

Some of these occasions may be chalked up to your child taking the micky: they heard you loud and clear but decided they would live dangerously today. Some of them may be because **they're in the *flow* of the game.**

Flow is a state of mind that games can produce – and aim to produce – in a player that elicits feelings of elation, and the player becomes highly focused and narrows in on what they're doing.

Most importantly, flow is associated with the distortion of time. Fancy way of saying children get in the zone and lose track of time.

The secret to flow

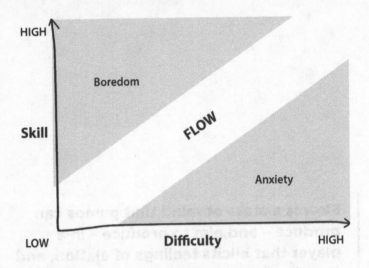

Games developers create flow by designing a game to be easy and require little skill at the start, and then they slowly step it up.

If the game is too difficult to begin with, you get anxious about it and give up. If it requires too much skill or learning, you just get bored because you can't keep up. So, once you're drawn in at the entry level, they slowly increase the difficulty and skill level required.

Once upon a time, this was done by games having levels built into them. You might recall old arcade games or early fighting games having a level and a big challenge at the end. Once you passed that level, you unlocked the next one. Modern games do this in far more sophisticated ways, but the concept remains the same.

The power of flow on an adult

Many years ago, I used to take the train to work a few days a week. It was around the same time I quit all social media for 6 months – you know, practise what you preach and all that. I listened to music and people-watched on my train rides.

There was one woman who would get on my train every day and play the popular game app Candy Crush. For those of you playing along at home that are not familiar, it's a game where you pair together differently coloured candy objects to make combinations and get points. There are time limits to each level and it gets more difficult as you go. The perfect example of flow.

This woman would play Candy Crush every day for the 20 or so minutes the train rattled on. She wouldn't let anything interrupt her flow. **She had a laser-like focus that would drown out any distraction** like a noisy cougher on the carriage, a crying baby and, most days, the train doors opening at her stop.

Seriously, it was a running joke with my wife, and I would text her updates each morning to let her know if the Candy Crusher remembered her stop. I didn't keep a running tally, but I'd guess she made it off less than 50 per cent of the time.

TRY THIS QUICK EXPERIMENT

Have a quick think about the last time you caught public transport. Train, bus, tram, plane – it doesn't matter. **Can you tell me three things about a person you noticed on that trip?** It might be what they were wearing, doing or a conversation they were having.

1. _____

2. _____

3. _____

If you're drawing a blank, don't worry, you wouldn't be alone.

Next time you catch public transport, try and last the entire trip without checking your phone or any other device. Just observe what others are doing.

How many people are in a trance to the point of not noticing a single thing around them?

How many of them are in their flow?

PSYCH SCIENCE #3:

The near-miss effect

Ever played a game where you got so close to winning or finishing a certain part but you fell agonisingly short?

Humans usually interpret this as 'I was so close. I'll go again. I've got it this time'. This is called the 'near-miss effect', or the 'fun failure effect'.

Games are not designed for you to start, get 10 seconds in and then die.

Perhaps I should rephrase that. Well-designed games aren't designed that way. **They want to encourage you, give you some hope that you're not a complete failure.**

Top marks if you noticed this is closely linked to the previous concept of flow.

The near-miss effect is a common theme in gambling research.

The idea that, for example, a poker machine will spin and deliver the punter a 'King, King, King, King, Queen! Ohhhhh, I was so close!'

> **Rather than interpreting that as a failure and a loss, we think of it as being <u>close to winning</u>.**

The reward centre in our brain fires off and it's exciting! We shove more money in and hit the button again.

It's a similar scenario if you're gambling on table games like roulette. **You attribute a near miss to somehow equalling better odds on the next spin, even though mathematically the odds don't change.**

This is not a new concept. It's been present in gaming for a long time.

Old-school games benefited from this, but perhaps not in an intentional way. What I mean is, it would be taking place as I tried to win at Mario Kart on Nintendo 64, but I don't believe it was a well-thought-out or intentional process by the game designer back then.

In modern games, the near-miss effect is a core feature.

If you asked your child or teenager if you could play a round of their chosen game with them, and in the rare event they granted you that privilege, you'd be surprised that **most games will be able to detect you're a novice.**

They may detect this through your poor choice of moves or simply because you're playing as a new account or character. What happens next is your child moans that you're getting somewhere due to blind luck, and after a reasonable amount of time your character will die.

Your child will tell you the outcome of the game is based purely on skill. There is some truth to that.

But most games use algorithms that lean into the near-miss effect, which means everyone feels like a winner!

I'm not saying we all fall just short. But if you're a legitimately terrible first-time player and you actually make a game of it, you'll feel encouraged to keep going.

Let's talk real-world stuff.

The near-miss effect visits your house something like this:

> **You**: 'Get off the computer. You need to go to bed.'
>
> **Teen**: 'Yeah, yeah, this game finishes in 4 minutes and 33 seconds.' (Points to the timer on the screen, which is meaningless to you – it may as well be last night's Lotto numbers for all you know.)
>
> Ten minutes later ...
>
> **You**: 'What on earth are you doing! Is that a new game?'

Your child had every intention of getting off after that game. But once she'd finished that last game ranked 4th out of 100 players, she felt like she was so close to that first career win, she was on a roll!

At the same time, she was put up on a leaderboard of the top 10 players showcased in front of her mates, with flashing lights and music playing like she'd just won gold at the Sydney Olympics.

The near-miss effect takes over and your teenager hits the button to play again.

PSYCH SCIENCE #4:

The dopamine effect

This is going to be a tough one. It's complicated. But rather than drag you along with me, I'll politely apologise to all the neurologists, neuropsychologists and any other iteration of 'neuro' profession at the outset. Look away now; this won't be written in an academically pleasing fashion. **I don't want parents skimming over this section, because it's super important.**

> **In my experience, parents who understand this part are far more likely to put my Tech Diet into action and are far more successful at applying it.**

Dopamine is a chemical in the brain that makes us feel good. It's in a whole host of awesome stuff like sugar and chocolate. Well, it's not actually IN the chocolate, but it's the chemical that goes off in your brain to tell you that you're eating something downright delicious.

While chocolate and sugar are not good for you, in moderation they're okay. Dopamine is also connected to things like gambling, drugs and sex. Of course, dopamine is the 'good feeling' part of those things. And anything that feels *that* good usually comes with some negatives.

You may be aware **there is increasing evidence that dopamine goes off in the brain when gaming.** The science is still early in its development, but most of it uses functional magnetic resonance imaging (fMRI), another term for a fancy picture of your brain. They measure the parts of your brain that light up and amounts of chemicals like dopamine, to see what, if any, impact playing a game can have.

In my opinion, there is a huge amount we haven't even looked into, and the small amount of research that has been done in the last 5 to 10 years struggles to catch up with how quickly technology moves. For example, we have studies on games that are a few years old, but those studies and data may be wrong once every child is gaming using a Virtual Reality (VR) headset, which is becoming increasingly popular.

If you just threw the book down and took a break, I know, it's frustrating. We can't keep up. But here are some of the key points I take from the research available to us at this point in time.

Dopamine is relevant.

We can say with reasonable evidence that dopamine does go off in the brain when we game. It's therefore a reasonable assumption that **when we see anger outbursts, tantrums or whatever you want to call it when you ask your child to get off the game, some of that can be attributed to the withdrawal of dopamine.**

What's even more fun is that, in many cases, dopamine is delivered even when we lose a game!

Remember the last section about the near-miss effect? That's right, the chemical reaction is still occurring even when we come close but don't technically win.

Dopamine increases when you play socially.

One of the most common things I hear in my clinic, giving interviews or during school talks, is people saying something like, 'Mate, video games can't be addictive, I mean, I played them for years as a kid and I never had a problem!'

Some of the most interesting parts of the research are little nuances that people like me find fascinating. There's evidence that suggests we get a certain amount of dopamine when playing a video game, as explained in the previous point. But there's also evidence that suggests **we get more dopamine if we play socially against other players.**[2]

It doesn't actually matter if you're playing a group of your best mates from school or random guys the game paired you up with in Singapore. It all leads to more dopamine.

> **This is crucial: more dopamine goes to the brain when you play against others than when you play against a computer.**

What makes gaming more addictive or appealing now as opposed to 20 years ago?

For me, it's the connection made possible by the internet.

> **With that connection came the possibility to play games on larger servers against more people and, hence, more accessible dopamine.**

If you take a look back through the history of the internet providers in Australia, it does roughly match up.

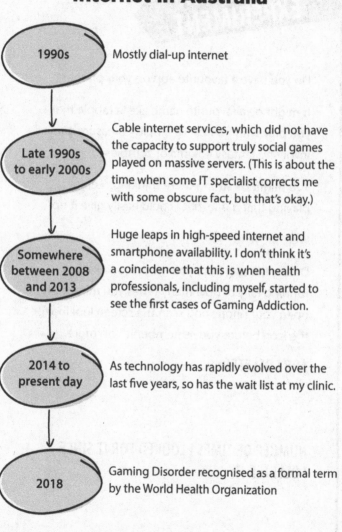

Internet in Australia

1990s — Mostly dial-up internet

Late 1990s to early 2000s — Cable internet services, which did not have the capacity to support truly social games played on massive servers. (This is about the time when some IT specialist corrects me with some obscure fact, but that's okay.)

Somewhere between 2008 and 2013 — Huge leaps in high-speed internet and smartphone availability. I don't think it's a coincidence that this is when health professionals, including myself, started to see the first cases of Gaming Addiction.

2014 to present day — As technology has rapidly evolved over the last five years, so has the wait list at my clinic.

2018 — Gaming Disorder recognised as a formal term by the World Health Organization

TRY THIS QUICK EXPERIMENT

Do you have a favourite app on your phone?

It might be a favourite game like Scrabble that you play with friends. Or a guilty pleasure game involving fantasy knights or zombies.

You might be sitting there thinking, 'I enjoy playing that game, but I could easily give it up.'

Well, prove it!

Delete the app from your phone and keep a running tally of how many times you mindlessly open your phone and scan the screen looking for the icon before you remember it's no more.

APP I DELETED:

NUMBER OF TIMES I LOOKED FOR IT SINCE I DELETED IT:

Impact on a child's brain

Please don't ask me what the impact is on a child's future brain development.

1   I'm not intelligent enough to know that. I'll leave that question to the academics.

2   If I did stumble across that, I'm pretty sure I'd be nominated for a Nobel Prize.

What I can tell you is that the research is pointing in the direction that the parts of the brain that are lighting up while gaming are the back parts associated with being in survival or fight/flight mode. Perhaps they're the best sections of the brain for thinking quickly and succeeding at these games.

More importantly, it means that when you're gaming, you're not completely using the front part of the brain (prefrontal cortex) associated with more rational thinking, emotion control, impulse control, and the list goes on.

Bottom line

This is more evidence that **when you turn off your child's game in a full-blown meltdown, it could take them up to 30 minutes to come back to a reasonable state.** And let's face it, teenagers are not always the most reasonable people even when calm.

Let's get one thing straight: social media is a modern form of communication that can be great.

But, at its worst, it can have a damaging effect on your child's self-esteem.

CHAPTER 3

THE PSYCH SCIENCE OF SOCIAL MEDIA

What's your social media IQ?

I can't cover all things social media and online safety in one book. There are many books and resources on those topics that I encourage you to read.

I sense a collective sigh from parents who just thought, *I bought this book for him to tell me what social media is? Seriously?*

Two quick points:

1   **Many parents don't understand social media in the way that their kids do.**

2   **Some who think they understand also believe: 'It's only Facebook, right?'**

When I was studying in the USA, I was one of the lucky few to be blessed with Facebook arriving at my college first. I was on the front line back when Facebook was called 'The Facebook'. I feel like such a pioneer. It's basically my claim to fame. *Yes, I'm being sarcastic.*

In fact, on the few occasions I've rolled that story out to teenagers in my clinic, they give me that look you get when you've just told the world's worst dad joke.

The Yellow Social Media Report 2018 provides us with the most up-to-date stats on how we Aussies interact with social media.

As a nation, we use social media platforms including:

Facebook (91%)

YouTube (53%)

Instagram (39%)

Snapchat (23%)

LinkedIn (22%)

Twitter (19%)

These are platforms used to post or view content posted by others. They're often linked, but different from, social media messaging services used purely to communicate.

As a nation, we use messaging service platforms including:

Facebook Messenger (79%)

WhatsApp (34%)

Viber (15%)

If you don't use messaging services, think of them as the new age text messaging. (This is not me going all 'IT talk' on you.)

This is really important when implementing your Tech Diet because these messaging services require the internet or Wi-Fi to operate, which of course is different from traditional text messaging that uses phone networks.

The statistics above are for adults (aged 18+), which is problematic. We don't have robust data in Australia that drills down that deep on child and teen use. However, in 2015 a large study found that **10 per cent of Australian teenagers use the internet for more than 9 hours per weekday.**[3]

Now that you've been briefly wowed (or bored) by statistics, let me tell you the trends I see in my clinic.

First things first: online safety for children and teenagers is crucial, particularly when using social media.

Top three trends I see:

1 **The age of screen and internet use is getting younger.** That is, the number of 8- to 12-year-olds that have access to social media, messaging services and smartphones is increasing.

2 **Teenagers are now more likely to use Instagram and Snapchat than Facebook.** Most teenagers tell me that they have accounts on all of them but lean towards certain platforms. There certainly is a school of thought, which is endorsed by many teenagers, that they avoid Facebook because it's populated by dorky adults.

3 **Young girls often spend more time on social media, and boys more time gaming.** However, boys in the last few years have been increasing their use of social messaging services like Snapchat.

PSYCH SCIENCE #5:

The hyper-personal effect

The hyper-personal effect is another fancy-named concept that's really commonsense. It refers to the idea that **any comment made online has more emotional power or pull than one made in person.**

I see this day in, day out in my office. **Teenagers will rarely be bothered by a face-to-face altercation or disagreement that happens at school when compared to one that occurs online.** It can be easy for us parents to assume this all occurs on 'The Facebook', but it's more likely to be in a group chat session on a messaging platform.

Again, it's not rocket science. Any comment made in a group setting with teenagers physically standing around is limited to how many people can hear that comment. **That same comment made in a group chat can reach hundreds, instantly.**

Add in the fact we don't get the benefit of seeing how those people reacted. Are they laughing? Are they shocked? Are they disgusted? Our imagination is left to run wild about how that comment was received.

If you use WhatsApp, Viber, Facebook Messenger or even the archaic group email method, you've no doubt experienced this yourself. Any criticism or perceived criticism on these platforms can hit really hard.

You may have noticed I just used the word 'perceived' criticism because there is another complicating factor at play here. **When comments are made online, it's difficult to pick up on subtle human cues.** For example, was it said in good humour or with malice? When said in person, we can use body language and facial expressions to guide us, but online we're left trying to interpret the emoji (funny face) or GIF (magical moving picture inserted in a message) that goes along with the comment.

Let's boil this one down.

Young children and teenagers don't come hard-wired to deal with big emotions. It's something they're learning – some quicker than others. So it's logical to suggest when the hyper-personal effect kicks in they're more prone to become upset or angry about comments made online.

PSYCH SCIENCE #6:

Social comparison theory

This concept is fairly well known and has received some media attention in recent years, helping educate us all. It refers to the idea that **we compare ourselves – our self-worth and self-esteem – in relation to the successes and failures of others.**

Okay, smart psychobabble guy, people have been doing that since the dawn of time! Absolutely correct. It's human nature to do this.

What's that got to do with screens?

I'm no history professor but I'm pretty sure hundreds of years ago we all went to a dinner party and bragged about our achievements while strategically steering clear of our failures.

How many times have you heard that technology has made the world smaller? In the 1980s I can remember my mother listening to cassette tapes of her twin sister in the USA updating her about all the family from her homeland. This isn't one of those heartfelt 'poor me' growing-up stories – we did okay. My parents were, and still are, incredibly frugal people who couldn't justify paying $3 per minute for a landline phone call to the USA. Fast-forward 30 years and my mother has only just grasped the concept that she can video-chat with her twin sister – for free!

Back to the social comparison theory. My mother was comparing her life to that of her twin (the ultimate competitive benchmark for a human, I've learned) in a way that would take months to get feedback. Technology and the wonderful world of the internet mean we get this on tap. Every second, if not every minute. And **people are not very honest about what they put online – you only see the glamorous side.**

Let's talk about how this can trap your teenager.

Have you heard your teenager moan something like, 'This is crap – we go on holidays to this sh*tty beach up north while all my friends are in Fiji!'

Chances are they have seen a photo on social media of their friend's 'perfect' holiday spot. The picturesque beach only shown in postcards. This is how a teenager will interpret that post, usually on face value.

Some of us with more experience and slightly more developed brains (adults) can, on occasion, rationalise and see the mirage. **The unedited, unfiltered version of that photo may contain some stray dog who just pooped next to your beach chair**, a terrible sunburn or even rain clouds that have been expertly hidden.

Or better still, the teenager who posted the above photo complains to her parents, 'I don't want to be on this stupid holiday in Fiji. I should be at home with my friends,' after seeing a post from friends who've visited an amazing new dessert bar and taken a group selfie.

Of course, that post glosses over the $23 they had to pay for the privilege, the 35-minute queue at the front door and the two stinking hot buses it took to get there. No, your teenager doesn't see any of that in the post, only the glamour.

There have been several Instagram and other social media 'celebrities' (I use that term loosely) who've come out to provide details about what is really involved in those pictures and posts. The summary being, those pictures posted online by influencers typically involve hours of makeup, hair, lighting, professional photographers, etc. – all to take one photo. Yet that is the photo adults and kids are using to judge their own success or failure.

I've seen this concept crush the self-esteem of once-confident teenagers.

Not quite as it seems

Carrying on with what appears to be a theme of me telling you how I've failed my own teachings from time to time, this is a picture of me and my daughter. I posted it to social media with some brag tag about my local beach.

 It's not hard to see why it could make someone think, 'Look at them, why can't my toddler sit still and ponder world peace with me?' Or, 'That's the most perfect spot, look how happy they are!' Often, we're not very aware of these thoughts – they're done on autopilot.

Hold onto your hats, folks. That post was a lie.

There was nothing picturesque or 'Brady Bunch' about it. The truth is, 20 minutes earlier we were trying to enjoy a meal in the restaurant nearby and my 'perfect' child decided I was a terrible parent because I wouldn't let her put hot sauce on her dinner. There was an almighty meltdown and out of courtesy – and my own embarrassment – I marched her outside to the nearest seat.

PSYCH SCIENCE #7:

The Zeigarnik effect

The Zeigarnik effect, based on research published by Lithuanian-born psychologist and psychiatrist Bluma Zeigarnik in 1927, refers to the phenomenon that **as humans, we are social beings and seek out a logical and satisfying conclusion to any social interaction we have.**

In real-world terms, if you're sitting down for a coffee with a friend and mid-conversation they abruptly stand up and walk out the door, how would you react? You'd likely walk after them, or perhaps stay seated while trying to make sense of what on earth just took place. What you wouldn't do is say to yourself, 'Oh, okay, he had to go. I guess I'll head to the gym now.'

Have you ever sent a text or group chat message and caught yourself checking constantly for a reply, saying something to yourself like, *What the heck is that guy's problem, he read my message at 10.42 am and still no reply?!* I think many of us have.

And teenagers are even more vulnerable to this, which is partly explained by the Zeigarnik effect.

How technology plays on the Zeigarnik effect

1 **The messaging feature that tells us if/when it has been read.** We start to crave that logical conclusion to our comment, post or question.

2 **Push notifications.** Those red icons that tell you how far behind you are in reading your messages or social media posts, and other kinds of alerts all play on this idea.

3 **Format of many social media posts.** Remember when social media didn't collapse posts? It was just one long scroll of the post/picture and then all the comments after it.

Now, most platforms make you click on an icon to expand more comments. Typically, this results in us reading the last post first, then clicking multiple times to backtrack through the conversation to put the pieces of the puzzle together. Before you know it, you've just spent 10 minutes reading 34 comments from people you don't know about someone's new dog that you actually think is pretty unfortunate looking.

TRY THIS QUICK EXPERIMENT

Note: This one is a touch on the mean side, so please use it sparingly and ensure family and friends don't become distressed.

Next time you receive a text message or instant message from a friend, have a read. Respond with a short (but not rude) message before cutting yourself off mid-sentence. Something like, 'Hey mate, good to hear from you, I think it's a good . . .'

Wait an hour or two and if they haven't responded yet with frantic confusion trying to draw a social conclusion, message them again with something unrelated.

Most people will try to abruptly or politely steer you back to the original conversation so they can get the logical conclusion they crave.

WHO I MESSAGED:

WHAT I MESSAGED:

RESPONSE:

Fake Instagram (AKA Finstagram)

It would be neglectful if I closed out a chapter on social media without mentioning the common trend among teenagers – and political operatives in foreign countries! – to use fake social media accounts. The term 'Finsta' or 'Finstagram' became popular around 2014 when that ever-reliable source known as the Urban Dictionary alerted the adults of the world to the fact that this wasn't just an anomaly reserved for those trying to catfish (build a fake profile to trick an unsuspecting person), but it was now widely used by teens.

If you laid the ground rules when your teen first asked for social media accounts and claimed proudly to your partner, 'Don't worry, honey. **I laid down the law. I told her she has to give us full access with her password to her account and we'll do random spot checks**,' while standing under a banner claiming 'parent win' and imagining fireworks going off in the background.

I'm sorry, your teen has likely had the last laugh.

Finsta is not just used on Instagram. It's for any social media or messaging platform. And if you haven't put the pieces together yet, I'll spell it out.

Your teenager has a social media profile likely using his/her actual name like 'Sarah Roberts'. It has perfect angel photos of her and all the messages in there are tasteful and above board. This is the profile your teenager will use to friend Aunty Gladys who she knows full well spends way too much time online and will call you at the first sign of anything inappropriate. **This is the profile you tactfully negotiated to have the password to.**

There is, of course, a second profile. Something named close enough her friends know it's her, but not so close that parents can search and easily find it. Perhaps 'Sa-rah Robs'. Okay, so I'm not as creatively blessed as teenagers, but you get the point. In some instances, this account may be completely fine and it's just your teenager's way of rebelling against your attempted control. On the other hand, **this typically is where inappropriate photos, posts and messages are shared.**

It's not uncommon to have groups of friends who know which profile they should use to post and message stuff that parents wouldn't approve of. At the same time, teenagers will often give their friends a helping hand by posting parent-friendly material to the original account to throw parents off their scent.

What to do if your teenager might have a Finsta account.

It's best not to come in guns blazing. **If you start throwing around accusations with no evidence, the argument usually descends into chaos** and ends with you accused of being 'the worst parent in the world' or some version of that.

Consider raising it in general conversation. It will go something like this:

> **You**:   'You know, I read online today that some kids have fake social media accounts to fool their parents.'
>
> **Teen**:   'Yeah, interesting. Thanks for that.' (Rolling eyes.)
>
> **You**:   'Do you have any friends or anyone at school that does that? Seems like a waste of time to me. I don't get why you'd need to do that.'
>
> **Teen**:   'Nope, never heard of it. The article you read must be wrong.'
>
> **You**:   'Yeah, the article must have got that wrong, I guess. Seemed interesting though. Went into a lot of detail about how they do it.'

What does this achieve?

It's what I like to call a gentle shot over the bow without causing a full-blown argument.

It might have your teenager rethink using the account, or just be a little more mindful about what they're doing online because they'll have a nagging doubt you're onto them.

On the flip-side, if they don't have a Finsta account, they'll chalk it up to you making uncool parent small talk and move on.

Should I start spying on my kid's social media, messages or emails?

This is a tough question. I've heard professionals on cyber-safety recommend that parents get full access to their teenager's accounts and read their personal messages whenever they like.

I understand the rationale, but, in my experience, there is one major downside to this.

Trust. It erodes trust between a child and their parents instantly.

Ultimately, this is a decision for each parent.

For all parents who raise this in my clinic, I ask them this question: **if you find something really concerning, are you willing to approach your child or teenager with that information and be honest about how you obtained it?**

Because if not, I don't see the point of spying in the first place. It usually leaves you in a stand-off where you're accusing them of something using the information you found, and **they won't even engage in that conversation until you admit you broke their trust by spying on their personal device.**

It's a lose-lose situation.

I am about to introduce you to a
parallel universe – the shady world
of gambling on games.

Mainstream media has only touched
the surface in this area. Let's go deep.

CHAPTER 4

IS YOUR CHILD GAMBLING ONLINE?

Check your bank statement

When I'm at speaking engagements, **I ask parents for a show of hands if their children have gambled online.** The question is often met by some puzzled looks – clearly those parents who haven't come up against this before. Or perhaps those are the parents who just haven't caught their children, yet.

Please don't use that last line to hysterical proportions.

The Unplugged guy reckons our son went to an online casino last night. That's it! Throw the computer out – we're going off-grid! I knew you shouldn't have paid him $10 to wash the car. It's all your fault!

On the flip side, those parents who are not puzzled by the question furiously search for a pen and paper, hoping I'm going to give them a simple strategy to fix this.

> **The best way to guard against your child losing money or gambling online is to understand how it works.**

I'm not going to lie, it's a complicated topic. Like everything in this book, I'll attempt to break it down for you in the most parent-friendly, non-tech way possible.

In my work, I've found the easiest way to think about this topic is by breaking it into three main areas:

1 In-game purchases

2 Betting on games

3 Gambling online

Let's run through these main categories first, then I'll cover the common ways kids practically do this without drawing attention from pesky adults.

PARENTS' CHEAT DICTIONARY FOR GAMBLING LINGO IN ONLINE GAMES

READ THIS FIRST TO PREVENT MASS HYSTERIA AND CONFUSION IN THE NEXT SECTION.

Esports: A form of competition for video games or a general term for the 'professional' leagues of different video games.

First-person shooter: A type of game where the main objective is usually to kill the others, typically played from the perspective of your character, where your weapon is in front of the screen.

Gaming or digital platforms: A place you can purchase games that are downloaded directly to your device or streamed through that platform.

Loot box: A 'box' in game that you pay money to open – it gives you prizes, like a lucky dip at a kid's party. You might unlock a weapon, a character or in-game credit. Or you might get nothing.

Skins: A generic term for any item in a game. It could be a weapon, a piece of clothing, a shield.

Virtual currency: The token economy or money system used in a game or on a gaming platform.

In-game purchases

This is an area that has been gaining some media attention and public debate in the last few years. If you're not familiar, we're talking about all the optional extras you can pay for within apps and games. **In the sales world, this is akin to upselling.**

The upselling model first appeared in popular apps. You'd be playing along in your fantasy land that had us all building a farm or raising zombies or any number of variations, and you'd be allowed a certain amount of credit to play in a certain period. If your credit was up, a clock would appear on your screen and ask you to patiently wait 20 minutes, 60 minutes, 12 hours (yes, really!) until you could unlock the ability to play again.

But wait … There is, of course, the option to pay up and play immediately. You may have figured out this sounds like a familiar play on the Psych Science we discussed in Chapter 3. **Pay up and you can skip the wait time!**

Fast-forward and many modern games and apps apply similar principles. It's said that imitation is the highest form of flattery. I suppose they realised it works. And just to be clear, when I say 'works', I'm referring to the economic sales model. It makes money.

Games that are free to purchase or download

If they're not free, they're a bargain-basement price. It's not like the old days when you had to physically purchase the game at your local store for $119.95. **Giving these games away for a song, of course, means gaming developers must make their money elsewhere.** This usually takes the form of in-game purchases along the way to open up new levels, new characters or perhaps loot boxes.

Come on mate, you've lost me. What on earth is a 'loot box'?

Didn't you read the *Parents' Cheat Dictionary* at the start of this chapter? Okay, I'll humour you ...

'Loot box' is a general term for a lucky dip item within a game. You pay a small fee, usually a few dollars, to open one up and you hope you strike it rich. You could end up with a loot box that gives you a huge reward or an absolute dud. If they get dudded, your child will curse and scream while you contemplate if it's worth entering their room to see what the fuss is about.

Some people claim loot boxes are not very random. I'm not geek enough to know. But those people say game developers ensure you win enough decent prizes to keep coming back for more. After all, that's the best way to keep you buying them.

Virtual currency

This is another form of in-game purchasing that many parents would be familiar with. **Most modern games have an in-built currency or token economy system.** Some even come with their own exchange rate.

Parents around Australia would be able to tell me when there is a fantastic deal on purchasing in-game currency for their child's favourite game. They've no doubt been on the end of a conversation that goes something like this:

Kid: 'Mum, there's a massive sale on Alpha-Bucks right now; you can get 2000 Alpha-Bucks for only $19.95!'

You: 'That's wonderful news. Remind me why you need this though?'

Kid: 'GOD! I've been through this. It means I can buy the magical helmet of Zeldron, which will make me impossible to kill!'

You: (Thinking to yourself, *Did he get abducted by aliens?*)

Kid: 'It's only on sale until midnight tonight, West Coast American time, whenever that is.'

You: 'Does it come with a free set of steak knives?'

Okay, you get the point. I think I also proved my dad jokes are coming along pretty nicely.

In-game currency can often purchase items that are commonly known as 'skins', which genuinely help you in the game.

If all your friends have amazing skins, you're often at a distinct disadvantage. This leads to jealousy and social pressure to up your game with new items.

It can also be used to purchase items that are purely aesthetic. Like a cape, a pet or a brand-new pair of shoes that do … absolutely nothing. Now that's a statement that most kids around the world (and perhaps some adults) would disagree with strongly. Children and teenagers tell me they can spot a 'Newb' – someone new to the game – by their character's add-ons or skins. **If you have a stock standard character with no purchased add-ons, you're often targeted as easy pickings.** Hence, social pressure to up your appearance, even if you're pretty poor at the game.

> **It's not uncommon to see children as young as primary school age spending hundreds of dollars on a spending spree.**

How does it work?

The most common way parents get caught out by this is by having a credit or debit card on an account. If you agree your child can purchase a game online or through their gaming console, they'll likely ask you for the card and enter the details. These details are usually saved for 'your convenience'. Sometime later, your child or teenager is playing and gets asked to purchase an item, upgrade something or open a loot box. At that point, it's far too tempting to just click 'purchase' and worry about the consequences later.

> **I often hear younger children around primary school age tell me, 'I didn't know it was extra money.' I don't buy that. They usually know exactly what they're doing. But I do sympathise with the carrot that was dangled in front of them and the impulsive decision they made.**

Many children and teenagers tell me they bought a few small items, and once they realised it was going to show up on their parents' bank statement, they felt there was nothing to lose. **'I was going to get in trouble anyway, may as well keep going.'** This is often how an impulse purchase of $5 or $10 turns into hundreds.

Safeguard your cards.

1 **Password-protect all your tech accounts linked to credit cards.**

2 **If you agree to purchase something for your child, get them to bring up the payment screen and then ask them to leave the room while you enter your details and <u>ensure the box asking if you want to save payment details is not checked.</u>**

3 **Have a frank and straightforward conversation with your kids that if there are any in-game purchases on the account there will be consequences.** Don't wait until they plead the 'I didn't know I wasn't allowed to do that. You said I could buy the game, and I thought you knew that was part of it' defence. You know, because it's your fault for not specifying they shouldn't do that! (That's sarcasm, just in case you missed it.)

All of this is a great start but doesn't prevent your child from straight-up sneaking in your wallet and taking your details.

This is another one of those times when people will accuse me of being way over the top.

So let me be clear: it's not a common occurrence, but it does happen in a minority of cases.

> > If it does happen, you'll need to be more careful with where your cards are stored.
>
> > If it continues, cancel your cards and reorder them so you can at least start fresh. If the old cards are stored on certain accounts, they'll no longer work.

Betting on games

I first came across this about five years ago. It's steadily become more problematic and common since then. From what I can pin down, it started with a few of the bigger online first-person shooter games.

I often ask parent or corporate groups, 'How do you bet on games online?' Years ago, I wouldn't get a single person who knew the answer to that. These days, there are a few who have cracked it. I reply with my tongue firmly planted in my cheek, 'You just go down to your local betting establishment or pull out your mobile betting app, of course!'

Panic ensues among the parents before I quickly clarify.

The reason I say that is to illustrate an important point. **Betting on professional gaming is fairly mainstream.** You can find it under 'Esports' and place your bet as quickly as you can back Liverpool FC to win the Premier League title.

I'm not suggesting Australian kids have access to these accounts, and they certainly can't march into the local casino or betting agency without being asked for ID.

So how does one bet on gaming?

It's actually remarkably easy.

There are a host of third-party websites based in many off-shore countries that will allow you to place a bet using an item or skin you own within a game.

A CLOSER LOOK

Tom is a 14-year-old boy who plays online games, mostly with his friends. **Occasionally, if his mates are not online, he'll join random games.** While playing with people from overseas, he enjoys the banter with the other gamers. Their attention turns from a healthy rivalry to talk of a wager.

Tom and one of these gamers agree to bet one item or skin each on the next game. Winner takes both items. They log on to an agreed third-party site to formalise the wager.

Tom soon realises he's been hustled. The average gamer he bet with has now turned into some amazing professional who beats him comfortably.

Tom starts throwing things around his room and swearing over the headset.

———

Are you scratching your head right now thinking, 'What's the big deal? It's just an item in a game; it's not worth anything'?

Unfortunately, that's not the case. Any item in this world is worth as much as someone is willing to pay for it.

Many games employ a meaningful strategy to create a market for their virtual items or skins. If you make 1 million Bronze Swords available in the game, it's a common item and will likely have a small market value. However, if you only make 10, and the sword has some special ability or power attached to it, then it's rare and usually worth something.

Now, if you want to buy and sell this item online because that's your hobby, then go for your life. (I don't see it as any different from a younger version of myself collecting NBA cards. Anyone want to buy an Upper Deck Anfernee Hardaway Rookie Card? Been trying to sell it for years but turns out he just wasn't the Hall of Famer I thought he would be.)

So, Tom takes the item to the third-party website, they value it at US$28 and they match that with something of similar value to his counterpart. They shake on it. Or click the accept button and away we go.

The website or broker holds both items in trust and awards the winner with both items at the completion of the game.

Easy as that.

People don't pay real money for skins, you're making that up, mate!

Yeah, they do. Let me give you an example.

In 2018, a famous American pro-gamer who goes by the name of Skadoodle won a huge gaming tournament.

The day after the tournament a 'Dragon Lore AWP' skin hit the market. It was signed by Skadoodle (yeah, I don't understand how that can be done virtually but let's let that one go through to the keeper) and sold on the open market to a collector for US$61,000.

That's United States dollars. Not some virtual currency.

Real money.

Like I said, every item is worth as much as someone is willing to pay for it.

It's possible to bet on games you're not actually playing.

Using the same method, you can also bet on professional gamers playing halfway around the world. That might be betting on a certain player or team to win against their opponents, or to win an entire tournament. Follow the live-streaming, grab yourself some popcorn and strap in.

I don't know about you, but I can't see how this is fundamentally different from me placing a bet on my betting app and watching the game on TV.

You might be wondering about now if there are age restrictions on these websites. Perhaps they ask you to confirm you're over 18 years old to continue, or maybe they don't even bother. I'm not sure.

> **The reality is, whatever safety measures websites use to ensure children aren't betting aren't working, because I see it all too often.**

How does it work?

To gain a full appreciation for how betting on gaming works, you need to understand the world of gaming platforms.

Gaming platforms primarily sell games in a convenient and quick format. Just because your child has an account on a gaming platform doesn't mean they're betting or doing something bad. In fact, the overwhelming majority will be using the platform just like you use your iTunes or Netflix account.

So think of them like an iTunes account for gamers. Essentially, these platforms let you sign up for an account and, in exchange, you can purchase all types of games, items and skins on that platform.

You can buy them through a credit card or their own virtual currency.

Have you noticed a theme emerging here?

> **Games, apps, gaming or digital platforms – they all operate with their own currency. That's a key point parents have to wrap their heads around.**

When I see teenagers in my clinic who've spent money gambling online, typically they've done it unchecked for months or years without their parents' knowledge.

That's because it's not going to appear on your bank statement as: '06/03/2019 BETGAMINGSKIN $18.99'. It will be through one of the console or gaming platforms. It could even be done through PayPal into those accounts.

Teenagers will get creative with transferring the money through many accounts to ensure they can easily explain the charge that actually appears.

It's a complicated system. Some parents may question their child's ability to actually figure this out. I mean after all, if they can't organise themselves to throw away that half-eaten meat pie that has turned a shade of dark green sitting under their computer desk, how can they organise such an elaborate system?

Like the answer to so many questions in our wonderful world, there are plenty of YouTube tutorials that show them how, if their mates online haven't already.

What can you do?

I'm not asking parents to call in a forensic accountant for a full audit of the family books. **Just be vigilant.**

√ **Don't allow your account details to be charged without question**, even if the charge does look like something that could be legitimate.

√ **Look for common warning signs such as kids staying up late to watch professional gaming tournaments.** If your child is up at 2 am to watch the best of five series between two pro-gaming teams and is noticeably emotional at the time (if you're awake) or the next day, you should keep in the back of your mind that there's a possibility they had a wager on that game.

√ **Be aware many of the platforms sell gift cards.** I knew this was getting mainstream when I walked into a service station a few years ago to see them sitting right next to the Coles, Myer and Woolworths gift cards. Nothing surprises me anymore. If your child has money from a recent birthday or a different gift card from Christmas, probably best to ensure that's spent on other recreational things and not to purchase credit on a gaming platform. If they have a $50 voucher, they may purchase a game for $29.95, leaving them with $20 sitting in their account handy for any temptation that may crop up.

Gambling online

Now that you've come this far down the rabbit hole with me, we may as well cover the much rarer and most extreme category. We have covered the way in which it's possible to buy items within games and bet them against others. But that's not the only way you can bet online.

There are off-shore websites that are akin to a full-blown online casino. They allow you to bet using various gaming items or currency from the gaming platforms we just covered. Of course, they take a commission from the bets and the odds are slightly in their favour.

A happy punter can take their items and place them on a virtual coin flip game. Now, don't get me wrong, I lived for many years in Balmain in Sydney's inner west, home to some of the best Two-Up action you can find on Anzac Day. I've been known to put the occasional bet on. But we're talking about people doing this from the comfort of their own screen. And worse, your child doing this using the items they purchased in a game!

If the coin flip game isn't your thing, don't worry. There's something for everyone, including a lottery-style jackpot and a roulette wheel.

I've seen teenagers in my clinic who've made incredible amounts of money doing this, and then lost it all. Dozens of times this has been in the tens of thousands of dollars.

Most devastating are the times when teenagers become popular among their friends and known as a bit of guru at this. Their friends start to back them financially, literally handing over cash to get some of the action. It may start out with a small win, but at the end of the day, the house always wins. **It's absolutely soul-crushing to hear a teenager tell you they were dropped by their entire friendship group when they hit a bad streak and lost it all.**

Once again, I've no doubt there will be people saying I'm scaremongering by even writing a chapter like this. But **I can't tell you how many children or teenagers fall prey to gambling or betting online.**

In my experience, in-game purchasing is a fairly common problem for parents. Betting on games and gambling online less so. But for those who say it doesn't occur at all, consider this: most reports estimate that betting on skins is somewhere between a $2 billion and $20 billion industry per annum. Even if you take the conservative figure, **we're talking billions ... with a 'b'.** Are you trying to tell me none of that figure is attributed to gamers under the age of 18?

Some parents panic too early; others don't panic soon enough. That's not a criticism.

How can we expect parents to know when to act if we don't know the signs?

CHAPTER 5

WHEN SHOULD PARENTS PANIC?

How many hours of screen time are too many?

Now, ladies and gentlemen, that's the $64 million question.

But I don't know. That figure doesn't exist. We don't have the research or knowledge in this area to give us that answer.

If I'm honest, **I don't think there will ever be a one-size-fits-all model** where we're confidently told, 'Hey parents, 2 hours is fine for a 13-year-old, but 3 hours will rot his brain beyond repair!' or any other scale or version that's so specific.

There are screen guidelines for different age groups, but personally, I find them to be so general they don't really provide a concrete assessment of where your child is at.

Take a breath and let me try to give you the best answer I can.

As a psychologist working with children and teenagers, **I was trained to assess all young people based on the impact their symptoms have on their developmental milestones.** This model stands true for a teenager coming to see me because of depression as much as it does for internet or gaming overuse.

That makes it sound a lot more complex than it actually is. After years of trying to explain this to parents in my office and at parent talks, I think I've managed to boil this down to language that everyone can relate to. I'm going to guide you through the five main developmental domains that I look for in every child:

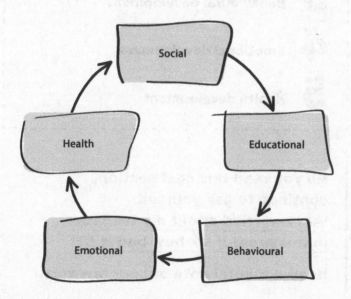

This section is the 'why'.

Understand why you should – or shouldn't – be concerned about that certain area of your child's development and you're far more likely to follow through with the Unplugged Steps that come later.

We'll use this model to assess how impacted your child or teenager is by their current internet and gaming use across the five developmental domains:

1 Social development

2 Educational development

3 Behavioural development

4 Emotional development

5 Health development

As you read this next section, continue to ask yourself: 'Am I worried about my teenager in this area? If so, how bad is it?'

Keep a mental note of your answers.

1. Social development

Whether you're concerned your teenager suffers from internet and gaming overuse or full-blown addiction, this is one of the primary areas that gets shaky.

I must say, I do find it ironic that in generations gone by, parents would be ringing alarm bells if their child socialised *too much*. Can you remember the days of arguing with your 'terrible parents' who wouldn't let you go to that huge party or complained, 'You're never home! It's time for a night off, just stay in tonight.' For many families right across Australia, this has now come full circle.

> **One of the most common things parents tell me is, 'He doesn't leave his room, I mean the kid doesn't have a social life anymore.'**

Of course, when I speak to their teenager they have a very different view. **Teenagers will argue until they're blue in the face that gaming and spending time in front of screens is social because they're doing it with friends.**

I encourage you not to fall for this. Don't get sucked in to this argument. It's a clever trap that many a parent has been tempted to enter but I warn you, it's an ambush. Run!

Okay, so don't physically run away, that's probably not helpful … **But don't enter an argument where your teenager won't be able to see your side, and you likely won't be able to understand theirs. Instead, accept their point of view, validate it and continue to stick firm with your boundaries.** It will go something like this:

You: 'For the seventh time, it's time to get off. You need to get out and see your friends.'

Teen: 'It's the weekend; I'm seeing my friends!' (While pointing to the video link of three mates all wearing headsets and screaming profanities.)

You: 'I understand this is where you like to hang out with your mates, and I'm okay with that. Just not all day. It's time to get off.'

Teen: 'You're the worst parent ever!' (While throwing the controller and storming off.)

I toned down that last response – I doubt it will actually be PG rated. It may seem strange, but to me that's a win.

Don't be fooled, there's no perfect Hollywood moment here where your teenager thanks you for telling them to get off, cleans her room, asks politely if she can help you with extra chores and then asks to ride her bike with the girl next door.

It's not too dissimilar to you being told by your parents you couldn't go to your third party in a row to see all your friends.

This is typically as good as it gets.

Let's get down to the nuts and bolts of social development.

Like any of the developmental domains, you must be careful when hitting the panic button.

Kids reach different developmental milestones at different times.

You may have a 13-year-old that still doesn't organise activities like going to the beach or movies with friends. I wouldn't say this is way out of keeping with kids their age. However, if you have an older child who did that at age 13 and doesn't now, you may assume it's a huge red flag. Remember: all kids hit these milestones at different times, and there is variance.

When I use the term 'social development', I'm referring to any age-appropriate activity that improves general social skills.

> **Any activity or interest that results in a dramatic decrease in a child's social activity will likely have an impact on their overall social development.**
>
> **It just so happens that gaming and screen overuse are pretty good at doing this.**

Where do children and teenagers gain their social skills?

Let's use some good old-fashioned commonsense.

> **Primary school-aged children** typically learn them from play dates with friends, going to school, team sports or activities, and family events. They may even pick up some social skills from playing with other kids in your neighbourhood ... if that still exists. This age is fairly structured in the fact that most of the time, parents or adults organise the activity.

> **High school-aged children (teenagers)** usually develop positive social skills from initiating their own events with friends starting with going to the movies, beach, shops, etc. As they get older, they graduate to large group gatherings and then eventually the dreaded party scene. They also develop social skills through attending school, family events, holidays and team sports.

This is by no means an exhaustive list of social activities you would expect from children and teenagers – I'm just pointing out the obvious ones.

A CLOSER LOOK

Michael is a 14-year-old boy in Year 8. **He is a slightly above-average student but doesn't put in much effort with his school work – in line with most boys his age.** He started gaming when he was nine. He played FIFA on his Xbox with his siblings and occasionally enjoyed beating his old man, who claimed the controller was broken to try and save face.

Michael has always been a talented sportsman, one of those gifted kids who could play any sport. His parents report he often played three or four sports at any one time in primary school and would have a host of parties and social events that went along with having that many mates. On the weekends, he would kick a footy in the street with some boys from next door.

Michael started playing a multiplayer first-person shooter game online when he started high school. He convinced his parents all the boys at school were playing and that it was a great way to make friends. He had some friends from his old school and sporting connections, but only a handful at his new school. His parents did notice this was a means for him to make new friends in Year 7, and he soon found himself in a new social group.

Midway through Year 7, Michael complained about playing too many sports and started dropping out of team sports. He said there wasn't enough time with all his homework from high school, which seemed like a logical argument to his parents. He gradually reduced to the point of only doing martial arts once per week at school, as mandatory mid-week sport.

During the recent school holidays, Michael spent increasing amounts of time gaming. His parents continued to encourage him – or nag, depending on which side of the fence you're on – to go outside, get active or see more friends. **Each time this descended into an argument as Michael explained that all his friends are online.**

This is a common story in my office.

So common, it's almost predictable now and I need to stop myself from finishing off the narrative when parents are talking. I'm not trying to sound smug about it. When I step back and think it through, the predictability scares me.

I'm not suggesting Michael's parents should force him to continue with his team sports. If he's genuinely uninterested in a sport or has out-grown it, that's fine. His parents should validate that he doesn't want to do that anymore and ask him to replace it with another sport.

One of two things will happen:

1 If he genuinely isn't enjoying it, he'll pick up a new sport.

2 If he was just saying that to free up more time to spend online, he'll likely get angry, then reluctantly accept that you called his bluff and you won't hear about it ... until the next time he feels he has the basis for a new argument and has another crack!

Michael is half right.
Most of his friends *are* online.

When I'm asked to talk to pastoral care staff and teachers at schools, I often find myself encouraging them to do anything they can to promote a school-wide or community-based solution. What I mean is **if we, as a community, band together to put reasonable limits on this, it will be a huge help to your child's friends and their parents in doing the same.**

If Michael had just two or three mates with similar boundaries imposed, they would likely contact each other and hang out.

> **There is no single catastrophic event in Michael's story. There are a series of small warning signs.**

When you look back on his story, he essentially reduced his social contact – sports, family time, friends – and had these social needs met online through gaming. Many teenagers and perhaps many adults would argue this is not a problem.

I respectfully disagree.

I encourage parents to think ahead to the next stage in their teen's life.

If your child's real-world or face-to-face social development is replaced during the teenage years, think of all the social challenges that lie ahead for them.

> How will your child manage in that first job interview when they have to sit in front of a formidable figure while questions are being fired off?

> Are they being interviewed on the content of the answers?

> Or the eye contact, small talk and body language your teen has learned during years of socialising?

I can tell you what I look for when hiring staff at my clinic. Perfect answers alone won't land you the job.

⚠ WARNING SIGNS
Social development

Not an exhaustive list, but some common red flags I see:

- **Dropping out of team sports**

- **Avoiding going to any family events**

- **Distancing themselves from old friendship groups and not replacing them with new ones**

- **Older teens not going out at all on the weekends**

- **Little or even no face-to-face contact with friends during school holidays**

- **Declining invitations from friends to hang out**

2. Educational development

Disclaimer. *(Another one – all this guy does is write disclaimers!)* I'm not a teacher or an educationalist. However, I do come from a family of teachers. (I considered asking my brother for help in this department but I'm not totally convinced he's not just a big kid in a suit and tie himself. Strangely, his primary school students really like him …)

Educational development is actually one of the easier areas for parents to keep track of and measure. And as I said previously, grades are just one aspect you should use to gauge this. I'm not of the view that achieving amazing academic results is that important. Some kids are gifted and will achieve this under their own steam, and all power to them. **Most kids need to be encouraged and praised for <u>effort</u> as opposed to results.**

If a parent tells me their teenager made a huge effort in a recent exam block, studying hard in the lead-up, **I suggest they reward them <u>before</u> the results come in.** Take them out for a special family meal and make a huge song and dance about the effort they put in. If you can build a child that keeps putting in work and making an effort, that's a terrific place to be.

Primary school-aged children:

> **Check report cards for grades and effort.**

> **Check in with your child's teacher to see how they're tracking.** I don't mean every week. That would likely lead to you getting a reputation in the staff room as 'that parent', which is not a great thing. In this age of political correctness, I find teachers are far more likely to provide parents with honest and accurate feedback when chatting in person or on the phone. That's not a criticism of teachers; I think we are all so protective and defensive about negative feedback, some of them have become shy about writing it on report cards.

High school-aged children:

> **Check the same things as for primary school-aged kids and then some.**

> **Other markers of educational development at this age include things such as:**

>> Not getting homework and assessments done on time

>> A dramatic drop in grades

>> Avoiding school altogether due to work not being done

A CLOSER LOOK

Taylor is a 16-year-old girl in Year 10. She's been an average student throughout primary school and high school. **She has always done her homework and assignments**, apart from the occasional mix up in line with being a disorganised teenager.

Taylor's parents had a **mid-year report that indicated a significant drop in her effort and grades.** To their knowledge, she's been studying and doing her work in her bedroom with the door closed – a typical feature most teenagers demand.

Her parents called the House Master and asked for further information. After consulting her individual teachers, the feedback appears consistent. **Taylor often forgets or doesn't do her homework and assessments. At times, she appears tired and lethargic, but this isn't every day.** She's very apologetic and hands her assessments in a few days late, which attracts penalties in her grade.

On reflection, Taylor's parents do comment that she's had a few days off this year with stomach aches and headaches and appears to then make a quick recovery before putting her head back in the books and saying she wants to 'get ahead'.

But it now appears she's been scrambling to catch up.

Taylor is not a bad student.

Her ability to achieve average grades didn't disappear overnight. When you look back, it's easy to pinpoint that she wasn't getting her work done. But this wasn't through lack of motivation, as she was clearly remorseful.

This is a common theme for teenagers who get distracted online while they're supposed to be doing school work. It's all too easy to get drawn in to the group chat or social media account that just keeps beeping at you.

I'm sure there are many parents who've struggled with this distraction themselves. Before you know it, Taylor's parents are knocking on the door to demand lights off and she's only done a fraction of what she was supposed to.

I've seen teenagers set their alarm for the middle of the night in an effort to catch up. Or, as is the case for Taylor, start to angle for a day off to catch up.

In extreme cases, this can lead to a cycle of school refusal. Essentially, that's a fancy term for not going to school for long periods, a few weeks or even months. It's certainly not uncommon for me to see teenagers who have missed entire school terms or have sporadic attendance of perhaps 60 to 70 per cent days off throughout a school year.

Traditionally in my profession, we have thought of school refusal as something reserved for extreme behavioural cases. Those teens who would skip school to head down to the local hangout, and perhaps even experiment with alcohol, drugs or other illegal activities.

These days, the majority that I see are more likely to avoid school to stay home, and **their school refusal is typically linked in some way to internet and gaming use.** Any teacher will tell you this can become a predictable cycle.

> **The more time they spend trying to catch up in class or taking days off, the more distracted they are and hence they're not absorbing the lesson of that day.**

⚠ WARNING SIGNS
Educational development

- Significant drop in grades

- Panic at night when it's bedtime and they haven't finished all their work

- Pattern of not completing homework or assessments on time

- Missing or avoiding days of school

3. Behavioural development

The one you've been waiting for.

The full-blown meltdown that has started to border on breaking stuff and getting violent. Well, that's this domain at its worst. It doesn't usually just flip a switch like that.

Like many of the developmental domains we're looking at, parents usually tell me this starts small and builds up.

> **A primary school-aged child** would typically have a tantrum or meltdown from time to time when they don't get their own way, no biggie. Unfortunately, that's normal.

> **For teenagers**, this becomes even more tricky. It's a stage of development where it's normal to question authority, especially that of parents, and is a natural path to develop into a healthy adult.

There's a difference between a child refusing to do what you or any adult, including their teacher, is asking, and one who then takes their behaviour to a new level. This can include verbal aggression – swearing and yelling. Or what my profession calls 'non-compliance' or 'oppositional behaviour', which again I find an odd term considering I'm yet to meet a child (including my own) who will happily do whatever you ask with a great big smile on their face.

Then there's the physical stuff. I usually break this down into two main categories:

1 **Property destruction**
A fancy catch-all term for breaking stuff. Anything. Their stuff, your stuff, the wall, great-grandma's vase that has been passed down for generations …

2 **Physical aggression**
Another catch-all term used to blanket any behaviour that physically hurts another. Punching, kicking, pushing, kung-fu roundhouse kicking (it's around this time you curse the thousands of dollars you spent on martial arts classes). You get the idea.

A CLOSER LOOK

Ryan is a 17-year-old boy in Year 11. **He was always strong-willed, even in primary school, but has never been in any significant trouble at school** apart from the odd detention and run-in for breaking a rule. Ryan's fairly insightful and calm. His parents report he's a personable, generally pleasant young man when chatting with family, friends and teachers.

Ryan threw tantrums in primary school when he didn't get his own way at home. His parents did their level best to not cave to the pressure but do concede they only followed through on occasions. When they were under work stress, they just couldn't muster the strength to argue with him and deal with the behaviour that would follow. At this age it would be screaming, the occasional swear word and crying.

As he went through high school, **his behaviour escalated. It was primarily triggered by arguments around getting off the computer and going to bed, or doing his homework before getting on the computer.** Once a week this would lead to him throwing things and punching holes in his bedroom wall. His parents would often find he had woken up at night to game, and Ryan would on occasion sneak outside his bedroom to grab his mobile phone, which was safely charging in the kitchen.

More recently, in the heat of the moment he is liable to push his mother or get into wrestling matches with his father whenever they try to implement boundaries around technology.

Ryan's neighbours became worried after hearing increasing noise, so they called the police. After several police calls by the neighbours and his parents, police have now started proceedings to seek an AVO against Ryan to protect his family.

I've been accused in the past of sensationalising this kind of case. The truth is, I don't need to.

I've seen a hundred Ryans. It's much more common than we like to believe. That's probably due to the fact that this kind of behaviour isn't exactly light conversation for the Christmas dinner table.

For those parents who are brave enough to speak candidly about it and seek help, <u>many say their family and friends don't truly believe what they're saying until they witness it themselves.</u>

In my experience, there's usually a pattern.

It doesn't just go from you letting your child game for a few hours over a week to this level of behaviour. The pattern also suggests that **the earlier you intervene with boundaries and a healthy Tech Diet, the better off you are.**

Let's be real. Would you rather deal with a 7-year-old having a meltdown and trying to get physical at home, or a 17-year-old with escalated, perhaps violent, behaviour?

I know it sounds cynical, but the latter is much bigger, stronger and can do a whole lot more damage.

Remember our chat earlier about dopamine? (If not, flick back to Chapter 2.) Dopamine, the wonder chemical that's delivered to the brain when gaming? **When you suddenly enforce limits on this after years of being pretty relaxed, you're likely to get a very angry young person.**

Please don't interpret that as me excusing this kind of aggressive or violent behaviour. I'm not. I'm simply saying we need to take that into account when we look at applying the Tech Diet.

⚠ WARNING SIGNS

Behavioural development

- **Increasing difficulty getting them to follow rules**
- **More frequent swearing and verbal aggression at home**
- **Increasingly or regularly breaking things at home**
- **Physical aggression of any kind**

4. Emotional development

Of all the developmental domains this is my least favourite.

Is this guy serious? Where did he get his psychology degree from? A cereal box?

Let me explain. It's my least favourite because it's the most difficult one to quantify with parents. As I've said before, **children and teenagers don't come hard-wired as experts in dealing with emotions.** So how are we supposed to know what is normal development in this area and what is a marker that something is amiss?

During our teenage years, we're hard at work trying to develop a whole bunch of skills like emotion regulation and distress tolerance and – I know, I promised I wouldn't go down the psychobabble route … I won't go on and bore you further.

These are important skills we need in order to be healthy adults that come as our brain develops and also through the hard knocks of experience.

It's, therefore, natural that teenagers will have ups and downs in their emotions.

Lucky you, parents! You signed up to be the punching bag for those emotions. Metaphorically that is. Not literally.

I've often pondered the impact that excessive use of screens, internet and games may have on a teenager's emotional development. It could be nothing and I'm barking up the wrong tree.

But is it that far-fetched for me to worry that a young person spending a large chunk of their time online in their bedroom may be missing some of these key life experiences that build emotional skills?

> **When gauging developmental domains, most of them will involve asking is it increasing in intensity and frequency?**

A CLOSER LOOK

David is a 15-year-old boy in Year 10. **He spends about 5 hours per day online gaming in his bedroom.** On top of that, he spends most waking hours looking at his phone, mostly on social media or watching YouTube because he's not keen on the gaming experience on such a small mobile screen.

He had a part-time job in retail, but that only lasted 3 months after he 'accidentally' missed some shifts to stay home and game. His grades are somewhat stable, but **his parents and teachers report he is lazy and just getting by on his intelligence.**

He plays for a school soccer team, but only to satisfy the school rules, and is able to miss most training sessions with a well-crafted combination of excuses around mystery illness, injury and forgetfulness.

David has become increasingly irritable and angry when asked to do simple tasks at home. He lashed out at a teacher when caught gaming in class, which resulted in him swearing and walking out of the class. There's a similar pattern developing at home, where he can be pleasant and nice to be around at times, then swing into anger and darker moods. His parents feel there's a pattern of this occurring when he lacks sleep or if he spends too much time isolated in his room.

Recently, David has had a falling-out with his friend group. It appears to have started over something minor, but he decided to remove himself from his mates at lunch and recess and now spends his time alone in the library.

Are you starting to see a pattern in my 'closer look' teens?

That's right, there are multiple areas of development impacted in each story. I'll go into this further in 'The domino effect' section that comes later in this chapter.

For now, let's focus on the emotional development of David. Many parts of his behaviour are stock-standard Teenager 101. The point of this is to highlight some of the more concerning parts that, for me, go a little further than average teenage emotional development.

> **When David experiences negative emotions – as all teenagers do – he has developed a reliance on isolating himself and picking up technology.**

Most teenagers will tell me, honestly, they feel this is a positive strategy because 'it worked, I calmed down and felt better'. And there's no denying they probably do feel better. But we have to ask ourselves: is this a positive way to cope with negative emotions?

Further to that, how are teenagers going to learn positive strategies for coping with negative emotions if they have a ready-made solution? Many that I see don't. Not in the short-term snapshot that I see, anyway.

> **Why would you listen to a parent, a mentor or someone like me suggest you 'go for a run to try and feel better when you're upset' when you have another method you feel works?**

There is another concern for David. His emotional outbursts appear to be getting worse and more frequent.

David is clearly struggling with the intensity of his emotions, which leads to his behaviour.

Remember those emotion regulation and distress tolerance skills I mentioned earlier? They would really come in handy for David right about now.

Every teenager – and many adults – has the occasional meltdown. That's life. **The difference here is the increase in intensity and frequency.**

I would guess many teenagers have been caught on their device or playing a game while in class. And if they haven't been caught, it's only because they're masters at flicking between screens. Schools do their best with firewalls and IT monitoring, but there are always ways around the system.

Your average student gets caught and is angry, mostly at themselves and the consequence to come, and will mutter something under their breath while the teacher dishes out the verdict.

⚠ WARNING SIGNS
Emotional development

- **Increasing frequency of emotional outbursts**
- **Increasing intensity of emotional outbursts**
- **Increase in duration it takes for them to calm down**

5. Health development

Health is not a developmental milestone as such. Although I like to think about it under that umbrella. When I use health as a gauge for how worried parents should be, I'm referring to everything from sleep and eating habits, all the way through to posture and personal hygiene.

Sleep

Sleep is sacred. I can't stress that enough.

Most sleep specialists say a child or teenager needs around 9 to 10 hours of solid sleep per night. Have you had that conversation with your child? How did it end?

Yeah, I thought so.

In my clinic, **I see a huge difference between teenagers that get 8-plus hours sleep and those on 6 or 7 hours.** Maybe it's just a magical number and my sample is skewed.

In my experience, when you dip below that 8-hour average it goes pear-shaped pretty quickly.

If you have a teenager who has a habit of telling you they're going to bed 'in just a few minutes, Dad', and then stays up until 2 am on a school night glued to a screen, that's a clear warning sign.

When I ask a teenager how many hours sleep they get, they tell me what I want to hear: '8 to 9 hours, Brad, every night.' **Whatever figure they give, I automatically take 30 to 90 minutes off for good measure and I arrive at a more accurate figure.** Teenagers know nothing good comes from that conversation.

Instead, I like to dance around the topic and figure out what time they get ready for bed, how long it takes them to get to sleep, and casually jump around what time they have to leave to get to school and therefore what time they wake up. Put all those pieces together and you're far more likely to land on an accurate account of sleep.

Anyone who works with or lives with a teenager will surely agree with the idea that getting any information out of them is much like putting together a complex jigsaw puzzle. Not like the six-piece one my young daughter has – I mastered that pretty quickly. I'm talking more like the 1000-piece puzzle you had at your grandmother's house that had a few pieces missing just to add to the excitement.

Your play should go a little something like this:

You: 'I'm going to bed; it's time for you to wind it up. You have school in the morning.'

Teen: 'Yep, I'm just saving my assignment now.' (AKA I'm in an intense group chat and I need to know how this *Days of Our Lives* type melodrama ends.)

You: 'No problem. If you're just saving your work, I'll wait 3 minutes so you can finish and then I'll turn the Wi-Fi off.'

Teen: 'You're so controlling. You treat me like a child!'

The early riser.

This is the other aspect you need to watch when it comes to getting a solid sleep.

I've seen an explosion of early risers recently, particularly among primary school-aged children.

They wake up at 5 am or 6 am, well before their mum and dad are awake, and sneak out to grab the tablet. Some will use an alarm clock; others are just natural risers.

Their usual defence? 'I woke up early and couldn't get back to sleep, and I didn't want to wake anyone else up.' So considerate of them!

Just do the math.

If your 8-year-old is getting to bed at 8.30 pm and waking up at 5 am or 6 am to game, they're falling well short of that magic 9 to 11 hours, which is even more important for this younger age group.

Later in this book, in the Unplugged Steps, I'll show you how to tackle this.

Exercise

Riddled throughout this book you'll see comments and references to the importance of exercise for children's and teenagers' development.

I can't stress enough how crucial exercise is.

At the most basic level, **exercise is something that will often be pushed aside if your child has a gaming or internet issue.** As I discussed before, it usually starts with excuses to avoid it or saying they don't enjoy it anymore and ends with an argument over taking the dog around the block when you've lowered your standards and will take anything that resembles some basic form of movement.

Now, I'm not going down the path of pretending I'm qualified to tell you how much exercise your child should be getting every week.

What I will say: the more exercise they do, the less time they'll be arguing about screens and the more likely they are to sleep well.

Nutrition

I'm most certainly not an authority on nutrition. I've been known to enjoy chocolate way too much, to the point where I have to ask my wife to hide her stash.

Most teenagers don't have the most ideal eating habits. I can recall a teenage version of myself splitting an entire loaf of white bread with my brother to make endless peanut butter toast. That was just afternoon tea before my parents arrived home. It was washed down with bottomless cups of Milo for good measure. So, there's nothing strange or abnormal about your teenager if they're avoiding the quinoa you left out as a snack.

The common warning signs in this area are primarily around:

> Rushing through meals to get back to their screens

> Refusing to eat meals with the family and instead take them into their room

> Most concerning, skipping meals altogether

Basically, if the screen is a higher priority than eating, you might have a problem on your hands.

TRY THIS QUICK EXPERIMENT

Offer your child dinner at their all-time favourite restaurant.

If they enter into solid negotiations about how long it will take, when they need to be home, and place their little sister on a timer to ensure they spend the least amount of time away from their computer as possible –

YOU MIGHT HAVE A MILD PROBLEM.

If they demand to bring their device along in order to minimise the downtime and stipulate that's the only way you'll have the privilege of paying for their favourite meal –

THAT'S PRETTY WORRYING.

If they flat out refuse, no questions asked, I'm not moving –

THAT'S HEADED DOWN THE SERIOUS END.

Posture

Bizarre. If you'd told me I'd need to warn parents of the muscular and posture symptoms presenting as a result of screen time, I probably would have doubled over laughing. Yet, here we are.

It's not uncommon for children who spend too much time on screens to present to their health professional – not me, I mean like an actual physiotherapist or chiropractor – **complaining of back, shoulder or finger problems.** My limited understanding is that it's often caused by poor posture. Shouldn't be a surprise really. Anyone who spends endless hours sitting in one position is prone to this, myself included.

After years of sitting for a living, I developed poor posture. I considered walking or standing during my consultations but for some odd reason that made people uncomfortable. That was another dad joke, I didn't actually do that. What I did do was purchase the most complicated back support chair you've ever seen. It does resemble the captain's chair from *Star Trek*, but hey, I'm a function-over-aesthetics kind of guy. Just ask my wife, she's constantly bugging me to put more thought into my poor fashion sense ...

Personal hygiene

If you read the heading and said, 'Oh, no! Our son's room stinks like a science experiment gone wrong crossed with a sweaty footy locker! There must be something wrong!' – unfortunately, that's fairly normal. Move along; nothing to see here.

In my experience, what's not normal is flat-out neglect of self-care. Refusing to perform the basics:

- ✕ shower
- ✕ wash
- ✕ go to the bathroom
- ✕ use deodorant
- ✕ brush your teeth
- ✕ that kind of thing ...

Self-care is typically refused not because they have some great aversion to it, but it simply takes time away from the screen.

As gaming creeps its way into the lives of younger kids (around age 5 to 10 years), I hear more parents complaining their child was toilet trained and has regressed. Essentially, kids so engrossed in gaming they don't have the presence of mind to read the cues of their bladder.

Again, never thought it would get this far ...

⚠ WARNING SIGNS
Health development

- **Secretive attempts to stay up late or waking up early to get online**

- **Avoiding sport or extra curricular activities to get on screens**

- **Refusing family meals or showering due to screen time**

A CLOSER LOOK

Daniel is a 14-year-old boy in Year 9. His parents have been mildly concerned about his internet use for some time and made some efforts to limit it. Every time they try this, **Daniel has raised the valid point that he needs the internet for his school work.** His parents found it difficult to argue with that, so they put parental controls or restrictions on what sites he could visit to ensure it's for purely educational use.

Daniel has been gaming for the last few years and he's decided he would like to be a professional gamer. He hasn't told his parents because he knows they won't approve, but he sees many successful professional gamers online making a handsome living doing what they love. He's joined a semi-professional team based in South Korea. The team auditioned him through a series of trial games, which he passed with flying colours. After all, Daniel is pretty handy at his chosen craft.

He starts feeling the pressure to stay up later even though he knows he's supposed to be in bed by 10 pm. Due to the time zone difference, the most ideal time for him to play with his team and conform to their social rules is between 8 pm and 2 am AEST. He's had some comments from teammates that he's not online enough with the team, so he starts to push his bedtime later and later.

Daniel's parents start to notice **he's tired in the morning and late for school most days. They also find him skipping meals and showers.** While they insist on school nights, come the weekend he argues it's his free time and wants to be left alone, so they back down. A few months later his father wakes up to get a drink of water and finds Daniel up at 2 am gaming.

Daniel's parents installed parental controls, so how was he gaming at 2 am?

It's so sweet when we parents use parental controls and naively think we've solved the problem.

I'm not saying it never works, but in my experience, **it's child's play for a savvy teenager to get around parental controls.**

I'll go into that in more detail in the Tech Diet chapter when I explain the Unplugged Steps.

I started this section by saying **sleep is sacred.**

Daniel's story is a fairly common example of how small changes in sleep can snowball quickly.

It's a slippery slope, and it's one of the first things that you need to look at when implementing a Tech Diet for your child or teenager.

The domino effect

The cruel thing about this effect is that when a child experiences one or two of these developmental domains being knocked around, it will domino. There are a million variations of how this can start and in what order it can domino. And many times, it's a case of bad luck.

Say, if your teenager stays up late and happens to have 'easy' classes the next day, they might be able to wing it with no huge impact. On the other hand, if their science teacher decided the next day was a great day for a pop quiz, it could snowball faster. Let me take you through a common example.

The domino effect in action

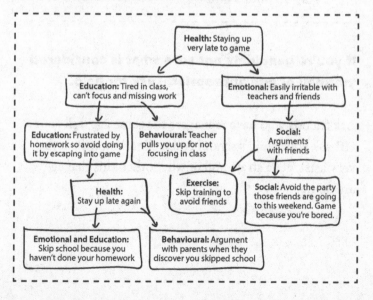

Putting it all together

Haven't you just described normal teenage behaviour?

That's a really tricky one.

At the start of this chapter, I did explain that we need to put it all in context. So let's recap with a concrete example:

> **It's normal** for a teenager to not want to go to bed on time and try to stay up late.

> **It's not normal** for a teenager to regularly stay up until 3 am.

If you're genuinely not sure what is considered 'normal' or age appropriate, ask for help.

Ask friends who have teenagers the same age, ask your GP, ask your child's school counsellor. You will, at the very least, get a straw poll of what other kids that age are doing.

Your turn

Here's your very own tick-a-box guide to some key areas under the five developmental domains that I recommend you watch out for.

I haven't tested this in some robust empirical study, so there's no magic number or cut-off that tells you your child has crossed the precipice from 'normal' to 'out of control'.

Use this checklist as a guide to gather your thoughts about how concerned you may be, and what the best course of action is from there.

Remember: you need to complete this keeping in mind the context of normal teenage behaviour.

Should I Panic? parent checklist

	Never happens	Has started to happen/ sometimes happens	Out of control
Using screens when he/she should be asleep?	☐	☐	☐
Getting less than the recommended amount of sleep on average?	☐	☐	☐
Skipping meals because he/she is too distracted?	☐	☐	☐
Dropping out of sports and activities without replacing them?	☐	☐	☐
Avoiding or skipping sports training or games to go online?	☐	☐	☐
Skipping showers or toilet breaks?	☐	☐	☐
Time online with friends over time in real life with friends?	☐	☐	☐
Little or no age-appropriate social events on weekends/school holidays?	☐	☐	☐

	Never happens	Has started to happen/ sometimes happens	Out of control
Significant drop in school grades?	☐	☐	☐
Regularly not finishing school work due to time spent online?	☐	☐	☐
Missing or avoiding days at school?	☐	☐	☐
Stolen money or ran up credit card to purchase items in a game or app?	☐	☐	☐
Stolen money or ran up credit card to gamble online?	☐	☐	☐
Frequently swearing or verbal aggression when asked to get off screens?	☐	☐	☐
Breaking or throwing things when asked to get off screens or when arguing about access?	☐	☐	☐
Physical aggression of any kind when asked to get off screens or when arguing about access?	☐	☐	☐
Increasing duration of emotional meltdowns when time online is limited?	☐	☐	☐

NB: This questionnaire should not be used as a diagnostic tool. It's merely designed to guide your level of concern.

Welcome to my favourite part of the book.

Enough with the stats and theory, let's talk about the practical steps you can take in your home today!

CHAPTER 6

THE TECH DIET

The hands-on nitty gritty stuff I get asked about every day

The Tech Diet is simple. <u>Balance.</u>

Enter all the parents rolling their eyes for another 'expert' stating the bleeding obvious …

In my clinic, I start off by assuring the teenager that **I don't agree with the cold turkey plan parents have often threatened. The reality is that it rarely works.**

Have you ever taken your teen on a detox by conveniently selecting a holiday location with zero Wi-Fi? If you're one of the rare parents who answered 'no' to that question, I bet it's crossed your mind!

In my experience, this can be temporary bliss, but all those Brady Bunch deep and meaningful chats are lost the minute you pull in to the driveway at home.

The Unplugged Steps are based on a list of core strategies or methods parents can use to encourage a healthy Tech Diet for children and teenagers.

The Tech Diet is based on the limited research and Psych Science outlined earlier, but most importantly, **it's based on the thousands of teenagers and families I've seen in my clinic over nearly a decade.** I've taken what works and thrown out what doesn't work in my hands-on clinical experience.

Let me be clear, once again: I don't describe myself as an academic.

These techniques are tried and tested.

And while I have no hard data or research paper summarising this – in hindsight that would have been really helpful to collect – **I can honestly tell you, if you follow the Unplugged Steps you have a very high chance of improving your child's Tech Diet.**

For those of you with younger children, around primary school age:

You have the luxury of being able to implement just a few of the Unplugged Steps and perhaps you'll choose to ignore the parts that don't sit right with your values as a parent.

That's fine! No judgement. I'm not out to parent all the children of Australia from a high horse.

I'll just preface that by saying the more of the Tech Diet you follow, the easier life will be for you when your child hits the beloved high school years and decides to communicate with you only through a series of grunts.

I recommend all parents implement the Tech Diet when children are in primary school before overuse has the chance to snowball.

For those of you with teenagers at home:

I hate to break it to you. **Most of you have little room for error when picking and choosing what parts of the Tech Diet you want to apply – you *should* follow all seven Unplugged Steps.**

You don't have to be perfect. In my experience, applying any new rules and boundaries with a teenager is seriously tough. Especially in those first few months.

But in general, I've found that the more parents water down the recipe, the more the likelihood of change dramatically reduces.

Important note before we dive into the concrete stuff

As you just read in Chapter 5: When Should Parents Panic?, **I don't gauge my concern for a teenager's Tech Diet based on the physical number of hours spent on a screen, but the impact it's having on their development.**

If you read Chapter 5 and had some concerns for your child in a few areas, or are just starting to see the warning signs, congratulations! You have some wiggle room when applying the Tech Diet, which allows you to be a sub-standard parent on the occasions you're just too tired to battle.

If you read that section and found yourself ticking multiple boxes in each developmental domain, then I would suggest **you don't have the luxury of picking which strategies to implement – you need them all.**

⚠ WARNING

The Unplugged Steps should not be read in isolation and implemented one at a time.

They're in a logical order to help chunk it down, but you should read ALL the steps, and then implement them one by one.

Reading them as a whole gives you a much better idea for what's to come and will save you making mistakes in the earlier steps.

UNPLUGGED STEP 1:

Control the Wi-Fi

Repeat after me: 'Without the internet, my child's games are useless.'

Remember the Psych Science stuff at the front of the book? That was pretty important.

If I told you to just simply turn off the Wi-Fi at home as a means of encouraging a healthy Tech Diet, you might try it for a day, maybe a week, and then forget about the Unplugged Psychologist altogether (while perhaps cursing my bad advice to your partner).

This is not a hypothetical. I've seen this in my clinic. I spend a significant amount of time just with the parents of every family I see. It's not because I need a break from the teenager grunting at me, it's by design.

I've found that **parents who understand the Psych Science are far more likely to understand why I'm asking them to implement this at home – and are far more successful at holding firm.**

So, to recap if you skipped the boring science stuff: **gaming without the internet provides less social interaction and less dopamine.** Therefore, for most kids, it's archaic and straight-up boring.

What do you mean 'control' the Wi-Fi?

Put simply, you need the ability to turn the internet or Wi-Fi connection on and off.

This will allow you to reframe **THE INTERNET AS A REWARD, NOT A RIGHT.**

I know this is easier said than done.

> If we can reframe the internet as a reward and not a right, then it becomes every parent's most powerful bargaining chip.

Gone are the days of pocket money being a tangible reward. Internet trumps this every time.

Don't believe me? Go and ask your child to do an extra chore this weekend. Not something simple that will take 5 minutes, I'm talking something that requires actual effort. **Now, test how much cold hard cash they need to be offered versus how much extra Wi-Fi time to get them to come to the party.** It'll go something like this:

You: 'Hey, Paul, I was thinking you could wash the cars this weekend. Thanks, mate.'

Teen: 'Nah, I'm busy, but I'm sure Dad will have time. He loves stuff like that.'

You: 'How about I pay you to do it?'

Teen: 'Nah, I'm good, thanks.' (While making a mental note of his recent birthday money earnings.)

You: 'How about I give you 2 hours extra Wi-Fi time after you do it?'

Teen: 'Make it 3 and you have a deal.'

You'll now use the internet as a reward for teenagers completing activities that we know as parents will encourage balance.

The classic example is a teenager who has been slowly avoiding exercise and sport. We know now that's important for general health, mood, sleep and learning social skills. So when Saturday morning rolls around and your child is starting the push back, which usually sounds something like:

> **Teen**: 'If you love the footy team so much, why don't you put the jersey on!'
>
> I suggest you calmly but firmly reply with something like:
>
> **You**: 'I can't make you go, but you have two choices. If you go, you'll get your X hours of internet tonight. If you don't, you'll have no internet. You pick.'
>
> And walk away.

The first few times you do this, they'll call your bluff.

It's not uncommon for teenagers to test out their parents' resolve.

Flick back to the *Should I Panic? parent checklist* in Chapter 5 (pages 130–1) to see the developmental domains you were most concerned about:

Where was your child struggling?

Where do you need to help them to re-establish balance?

Nuts and bolts of controlling the Wi-Fi

The old-school way of doing this was simply pulling the modem out of the wall. Effective, but it's a sledgehammer approach.

This is further complicated by parents feeling this is unfair on siblings who may be following the rules, as they'll then also be punished.

Ironically, there are various technological solutions that assist parents to manage Wi-Fi and internet access in a slightly easier way.

I have no financial interest in any of these products, but some of the families I see have used this technology:

✓ KoalaSafe

✓ Family Zone

✓ Parent Power

✓ Circle with Disney

✓ Norton Core

✓ And I'm sure there are more out there ...

Now, as you all know I am no tech genius, so it will be easy for me to explain this in plain English. These products work in similar ways (some slight tech differences) but all share two main features:

1. Turn access on and off.

They allow parents to create individual profiles for each member of the family. Your child and their devices are connected to this profile. **This allows you to turn internet access off and on for different children depending on their age, behaviour, and so on.** This is all managed through an app on your phone and is relatively easy to change on the fly.

So if your teenager has been gaming all day and come 6 pm decides Grandma's birthday celebration doesn't warrant their time, you're able to leave with the rest of the family in tow, pull out your phone and shut down their internet access as a consequence.

These products also typically allow you to set up timers and schedules. The most common use for that is the Wi-Fi being automatically shut off at bedtime. This is incredibly handy for parents who accidentally fall asleep on the lounge after a long day, and also for enforcing various bedtimes for different aged siblings. I don't believe they check if your child has brushed their teeth and tuck them in, but with the way technology is moving, I'm sure it won't be far off.

2. Parental control filters

They act as filters or controls for what your child is allowed to see. You're probably familiar with this concept – it's been around for years. Theoretically, if your child is supposed to be doing homework, the filter will lock them out of any fun stuff that could distract them. **In my experience, this feature is good for primary school-aged children, and mostly a waste of time for teenagers.**

It's not uncommon for teenagers to get around this feature by hacking the system or using a VPN (Virtual Private Network). Okay, I said I would keep it to plain English. Basically, while these products are very useful, in my experience, **you shouldn't assume they're flawless.**

The classic scenario is a parent installing parental controls at home, walking around feeling pretty impressed with him/herself and without a care in the world before … WHAT! How did you get on that? The truth is your child has been doing that for weeks but just didn't manage to switch screens quickly enough on this fateful day.

Children and teenagers are incredible hackers. They learn to code for fun, which is scary for a guy whose only understanding of coding is the green numbers that flashed everywhere in *The Matrix* series. I've seen teenagers bring down entire firewall systems at their school so they could casually relax in the school library gaming.

My point is, don't try to out-hack them.

> **The first feature we talked about is by far the most important one. Internet on, internet off.**

UNPLUGGED STEP 2:

Avoid Guerrilla Warfare

> Did you start out by taking or confiscating individual devices?

> Did you succeed in actually doing that for a sustained period?

It's incredibly difficult, but if you raised your hand to both of those questions then kudos!

Physically taking a device from a child or teenager is like asking them to part with an appendage. It usually ends in tears.

Most parents are able to keep this up for a short period (or for longer when your kids are younger). As your delightful child turns into a rebellious teen, this becomes a slog.

In my experience, **a large portion of conflict around technology comes from parents attempting to physically take a device.** This can be anything from swearing and yelling to breaking stuff (property destruction if you want to be technical), all the way to full-blown family and domestic violence.

Is this guy seriously suggesting I let my kid keep their device?!

Not exactly.

If you've already established rules in the house where kids have to hand in devices, and you're blessed with angel-compliant children who don't question this and still believe in the Easter Bunny, then by all means, don't give up ground.

What I'm saying is controlling the internet and the devices all without any objection is some kind of teenage utopia. But if this is not achievable, **put your energy into controlling the internet and trust that the devices are boring without it.**

I'm not suggesting this simple step avoids any aggression, conflict or tantrums. What I'm suggesting is that **turning the internet off remotely – even if you're in the house – is far less confrontational than entering into a tug-of-war with a device.**

A halfway measure

You could try not physically taking the devices, but establishing rules early on that they're not to be used in the bedroom. Again, no teenager will welcome this change, but if you establish it early on – during primary school – you have a much more solid base to work from.

Bottom line

If you control the Wi-Fi instead of taking away their device, you might still get the yelling or swearing but are less likely to have an explosive or violent situation that leads to the neighbours calling the police.

Why can't I just take his keyboard or controller?

This is just inviting a tit-for-tat guerrilla warfare conflict in your home. Most importantly, it rarely works.

I've seen teenagers in my clinic who laugh and even brag about their parents taking components of their device and how they got around it.

Yes, I know it's ironic that they just can't help but brag to me despite knowing that will be giving away some of their playbook … Ahhh, teenagers.

It's not uncommon to find them purchasing replacement pieces and storing them in their room so next time Mum or Dad march in and take the keyboard, hey presto! Problem solved.

> **Internet off** takes the guerrilla warfare out of play.

UNPLUGGED STEP 3:

Negotiate a Schedule

I'm willing to bet most parents have tried this. And failed.

Further, I'd say most don't know *why* their plan or schedule failed.

I'm about to break down the specific steps to negotiating a Tech Diet plan for your teenager. For those professional and corporate parents out there, you'll understand this well.

For anyone who is naive about the art of negotiating, we'll cover the two key rules.

Negotiating Rule #1:

You need to possess something the other party wants.

Light-bulb moments all around: *So that's why the first two Unplugged Steps make the internet a reward and not a right! I thought he just liked using fancy parenting language!*

Negotiating Rule #2:

They must walk away feeling like they've won.

No plan is not an option

While I've repeatedly said cold turkey doesn't work, there is one exception: **if your teenager is not willing to come to the negotiating table, the internet remains off.**

It's the only bargaining chip you have.

No plan is not an option. I've seen teenagers remain resolute for days or weeks without coming to the table, but **99 per cent will crack because you have something they want.**

What the hell do I do when they come to the table?

When I see teenagers in my clinic, my starting point is to establish how many hours of internet access they want per day.

I ask the teenager, who will no doubt throw out some ridiculous figure: 'I should have 6 hours a day because … <enter hilarious teenage logic here>'.

Teenage logic will range from telling you what their friends from school are allowed, quoting the UN's *Universal Declaration of Human Rights* or my personal favourite, 'There shouldn't be a limit. I'm managing it myself just fine.' Some teenagers are able to do this. If you're reading this book, that's clearly not your child.

Parents, you need to channel your inner salesperson when at the negotiating table.
If you think a reasonable amount of time is 3 hours per school night and 4 hours per weekend day, don't start with that figure.

Now, implement Negotiating Rule #2: **when negotiating with a teenager, they must walk away feeling like they've won.**

So start the bidding low, and I mean really low.

Some people get uncomfortable negotiating, but personally I find it quite easy and I largely have my father, Andy, to thank for that.

You see, when I was fresh out of university, I went to buy my first brand new car. Once I'd picked out my dream Mazda 3 with tinted windows in gun-metal grey, Andy leans over and says, 'Leave the negotiating to me.'

When it got down to talking money, he said confidently to the salesman, 'It's a great car, but we're not paying that price. We both know times are tough in this economy and if you don't sell cars by the end of the month you might be out of a job. So you need to drop it by $5000 and we'll take it. Go on, have a chat with your boss.'

My jaw hit the floor. **He wasn't rude about it, but I'd never seen negotiating like this.**

Of course, I didn't get the full $5000 off, but Andy explained later that he never expected to. It was just designed to set the bar low (but not so low he offended the poor salesman) and meet somewhere in the middle.

A realistic starting point

One tool I use with teenagers to get a realistic starting point is writing up their daily schedule on my office whiteboard.

I start with what time they go to bed – or what time their parents want them to go to bed – and what time they wake up. **Even the most oppositional teenager will struggle to argue they need at least 8 to 9 hours sleep per night.** Of course, the research indicates 9 to 10 hours is more appropriate but when you're at war with a tech-crazy teenager, I'll take anything over 8 hours.

Then I start plugging in their other commitments with them: school, sport, homework, shower, dinner, etc.

7 am:	Wake up
7.45 am:	Leave for school
8 am:	School
3.30 pm:	Sport training
5.30 pm:	Arrive home
5.30–9 pm:	Homework? Dinner? Leisure time?
9 pm:	Shower
9.30 pm:	Bed

Most of the activities on the schedule are difficult to debate.

So in this example you're left with 3 hours and 30 minutes to play with.

You then need to negotiate how much time dinner will take (30 minutes at least?) and homework (30 to 90 minutes dependent on their age).

What's left is the maximum amount of internet time that's physically possible. It's typically something like 1 to 3 hours per night.

Substantially different from the original demand: 'If I don't get 6 hours a day you're the worst parent ever!'

> You may have noticed that this schedule also focuses on a healthy balance with an emphasis on the five developmental domains being met first.

I don't typically ask families to make a schedule they will stick to by the minute.

For anyone who has tried to maintain a study schedule with a teenager, it's incredibly frustrating. Teenagers procrastinate and avoid studying despite having the times on the schedule.

What I do ask is that parents take that agreed final amount of 'free internet time' and stick to it.

So if the exercise highlights free time between 6.30 pm and 8.30 pm (2 hours) then **the Wi-Fi gets turned on for that period only.**

Note: This exercise needs to be done for three different scenarios:

1 School nights

2 Weekends

3 Holidays

I usually recommend you start with school nights as that's typically the time screens and gaming are causing the most conflict. You can then use this as a logical benchmark to negotiate the other days.

So, if you've all agreed that 2 hours per school night is reasonable, and you've specified that's going to be between 6.30 pm and 8.30 pm, you can springboard on to validate 'how horrible it is to be a teenager, and how you desperately need to relax on the weekends because school is so oppressive'. *Just in case you missed it, that was sarcasm.*

But in all seriousness, **do validate that they deserve some downtime on the weekends and holidays,** and you'll end up with something like 3 to 4 hours per day on those days.

REMEMBER: THE INTERNET IS A REWARD AND NOT A RIGHT.

This is your new mantra.

If you ever forget it, imagine yourself as a character in *The Wolf of Wall Street* movie singing it in a restaurant while beating your chest.

UNPLUGGED STEP 4:

Always Read the Fine Print

You may be shaking your head right now.

Seriously? This bloke thinks my kid should game for 3 to 4 hours a day?

As I've said many times, there's no golden formula that says 2 hours per day is a great Tech Diet, but 3 hours will rot your child's brain.

However, there is a catch in the fine print of my madness.

When I say 2 hours, I mean 2 hours. TOTAL.
(Or whatever the right number might be for your family.)

Internet on, internet off. That time includes homework, social media, gaming, YouTube, Netflix, whatever. I don't care what it is.

This is not designed to be a trick for teenagers. I tell them straight up. And you need to make sure they know that while negotiating the total amount.

But they need the internet for school work

Yes, absolutely they do. **Internet-based portals for homework and assignments are a mainstay these days in schools.**

I don't necessarily agree or disagree with this development, but sometime about 5 years ago, we as parents demanded schools integrate technology in the classroom. Schools responded by rolling this out urgently, some giving every boy and girl a device to call their own.

It was like an episode of *Oprah*: 'You get a tablet, and you get a tablet, and young lady you have one too!'

As I shared earlier, I don't think there was much thought about the possible side effects this would have. These have been well documented in the media of late, resulting in some schools banning phones and rolling back the tech trend at break-neck speed.

But enough about schools and technology, we are here to talk about your home.

The reason I wrap all internet use into one chunk of daily time is so that it's objective to measure, and it reduces debate.

Have you ever had a fight start something like this?

Teen: 'That's not fair, I wasn't really gaming, I was doing research for a history assignment – that doesn't count!'

It can be draining for parents to constantly debate the grey.

The Tech Diet aims to remove as much grey as possible.

A QUICK EXERCISE FOR YOU

When your teenager claims she needs 2 hours of internet per night for school work, I want you to contact their Year Coordinator, House Master or appropriate person at school and ask, 'Hey, Mr Smith, Alison says she needs 2 hours of internet per night for school work, what do you think an average Year 10 student needs per night in order to complete the work?'

THE ANSWER FROM THE SCHOOL:

I ask this question on a weekly basis, and most schools are happy to help.

They usually reply something like 20 to 60 minutes of internet for homework per night. Meaning large sections of homework can still be done offline.

The total amount of internet use per day you negotiate with your teenager will include homework and assignments.

<u>**This is crucial to note.**</u>

In the event they choose to game or do something else when they should be doing school work, they'll suffer the natural consequences at school.

If you're worried the school won't monitor this, I find sending the teachers a friendly email to explain what you're doing at home, and that you would encourage any feedback about incomplete work, will be an added layer of protection.

<u>**Make no mistake, work will be missed in the short term.**</u>

But this is the road to teaching teenagers a valuable lesson in managing their time.
Something that's vital for them to know how to do to flourish as an adult.

UNPLUGGED STEP 5:

Name Your Price

It's time to name your price. That is, as parents we've already identified our concerns around the five developmental domains: social, educational, behavioural, emotional and health. (See your *Should I Panic? parent checklist* answers on pages 130–1 for a quick refresher.)

In the following example, the teenager's parents were concerned that their son was growing apart from his friends, not exercising and was becoming aggressive in the home more often, so **they made their demands explicit. You need to do the same.**

You could probably see where I was headed with this in the earlier steps. If you're at the point of having a plan that's agreed by all, it might look something like this for a teenager:

7 am: Wake up

7.30 am: Leave for school

8.30 am: School

3.30 pm: Sport training

5.30 pm: Arrive home

5.30–6.30 pm: Homework

6.30 pm: Dinner

7–9 pm: Internet

9 pm: Shower

9.30 pm: Bed

My 3 Rules

1. No physical aggression
2. Must go to sport
3. Do homework first

If I don't do these, I'll lose 30 mins
of my internet time.

Maximum penalty: 24 hours

Break down your demands and rules into objective measures

When I say 'demands', I don't mean you should be rigid and lay down the law. That isn't usually a great way to get teenagers on board.

Instead, explain your concerns using observable and objective behaviour.

Hold up, Unplugged Guy. What on earth is that psychobabble? Observable and objective?

Let me break it down. **If you tell a teenager they have a bad attitude and they need to change it or you'll take time off their internet use, what are you actually asking them to do?**

I ask this question of parents constantly in my clinic.

It's not something that can be measured in black or white terms. Therefore, it's a hand grenade.

On the other hand, if you tell a teenager you'll take time off for any physical aggression in the house – hitting, kicking, punching, pushing, etc. – that they can understand.

One of my all-time favourite examples of this was a photo that ironically went viral on social media a few years back.

> The Wi-Fi password for today can be unlocked by sending a photo of your clean room to me. The photo needs to include your swimming trophy (to stop you from re-using an older photo).
>
> Thank you for playing.
>
> May the odds always be in your favour.
>
> Love, Mum

Three objective rules – max!

Back to our plan.

Now, develop some objective rules that you as parents want to see in order for your teenager to get their time. I typically ask parents not to pick any more than three.

Why?

Any more than that and they'll label you a dictator.

So choose wisely and prioritise.

I often hear parents say, 'Brad, he needs to bring the dirty plates out of his room – it's growing plant life and you could fall in love with an orangutan in there.'

Valid point. But as a parent, are you willing to prioritise that over his homework?

> **You can't tackle everything; pick your most important three.**

Maximum penalty: 24 hours. What's that about?

Well done, you spotted the fine print on the contract that was cleverly inserted in favour of your teenager.

Let me ask you a question: have you ever had a fight with your teenager that got so heated and out of control that you banned them from one or all of their devices for weeks or months?

If so, you're not alone. In my experience, it's difficult to enforce and follow through. We as parents get tired and have the inevitable conversation with our partner: 'It's been a month, right? I don't even know where I put the controller.'

When I ask children or teenagers about these huge punishments, 90 per cent of the time they can't tell me why they were banned. They've honestly and truly forgotten. 'I can't remember, man, I did something, but it was ages ago – it was like last week!'

Are they really learning the lesson once we get in that territory?

More importantly, this rule is in place because a teenager with nothing to lose is a dangerous teenager.

I can't stress this enough. A teenager with nothing to lose is a dangerous one.

If you ban them for long periods of time, you'd better strap yourself in because it's going to get rocky.

The 24-hour rule (or 48 hours for those parents who just can't bring themselves to be that lenient) is a guarantee to your teenager that **no matter how heated things get, you'll all wake up tomorrow and start again.**

This is important from an emotional development perspective.

> **Teenagers will make impulsive and irrational decisions. It's our job as parents to pull them up, but to also model healthy relationships where both sides calm down and move forward.**

UNPLUGGED STEP 6:

Minimise Mobile Data

Quick trip down memory lane. One of my first mobile phones was the Nokia 5110. It was an absolute brick of a phone but sat nicely in my Year 9 pencil case so I could text message in class and play the only game available: Snake.

I was recently listening to an interview with the founder of a major mobile gaming company. It was fascinating to hear how 'the other side' thinks about mobile gaming. Now, just for context, this is a billion-dollar business. And hats off to them for some serious business acumen.

The part that grabbed me was her passionately discussing the social aspect of their games, and how this had resulted in connecting people worldwide and even introduced people who later got married. Amazing.

For 95 per cent of us who have a healthy Tech Diet, that's ground-breaking stuff.

For the remaining 5 per cent, and for children particularly, these games can be designed to replace a developing social life.

Now some would argue that my last statement is false. That socialising online is the same as socialising in person.

I'm sorry, but that's ridiculous.

> How exactly does that develop the social skills required to go on your first date?
> Or go to your first job interview?
> Or manage complex social relationships as an adult?

It doesn't.

Okay, I got a little side-tracked by another rant that you can see hits a nerve …

Mobile data

Now that you have a Tech Diet plan in place, you've probably noticed that **there is a glaring loophole – your child's mobile phone data.**

Five years ago, this was a non-event. Easy for me to skip over because the average plan would provide something like 1 to 3MB per month. What does that mean? In non-technical jargon, it's an amount that's so small, your average teenager would burn through it in a few days.

I was walking through the shopping centre recently, chasing my daughter who was having a meltdown at the suggestion she go and have a chat with Santa about her Christmas list (that's a work in progress) and I stumbled across a mobile phone provider advertising 35GB of data for a $30 pre-paid mobile plan!

After bribing my daughter with a marshmallow (father of the year, I know) I popped in to chat to the salesperson. **This particular plan had incentives built in so when you recharge the next month, they give you bonus data.** What a deal.

Before you turn to your partner and scream, 'This goose had us implement that entire plan and now tells me it's useless!', let's think through the implications.

In general, **I find if parents give their child or teenager a mobile plan with zero data, their kids will be pretty unhappy. And rightfully so.** Most teenagers communicate through social media messaging.

If you're struggling with that, repeat after me: 'Text messaging and phone calling are ancient forms of communication last seen on Brad's Nokia 5110.'

> **I want your kids to have access to social messaging tools – it's how they'll organise social activities.**

At the same time, a teenager with a mobile data plan that allows them 10, 20, 30GB+ will find that **using the home Wi-Fi as a reward is a complete waste of time. It undermines the entire plan** as your child will weigh up, 'Should I do what Mum is asking? Ahhh whatever, I'll cop the consequence and just watch YouTube on my phone.'

Strategies to help you confront the mobile data monster:

> I'll give you a plan of attack for finding an appropriate mobile plan for your child

> I'll help you use the Screen Time feature on your child's smartphone to disable features and apps at certain times

I've noticed more recently that some savvy game developers have found themselves a gap in the market. **There is a new category of mobile game being released that effectively strips back the aspects of the game that chew through data, to make it accessible to people on limited data plans.** This throws another variable in the mix for parents trying to find balance.

Also, a shout out to the wonderful hotspot technology that allows you to tether a device to your mobile data. Amazing invention adding yet another variable as kids will use this to play on their traditional devices, consoles or laptops despite you controlling the home Wi-Fi.

Oh, and I forgot one. Telstra just developed a 5G network that, to my understanding, will bring us all leaps and bounds in mobile data speed and capacity.

Here's what you can do.

So you're saying we should buy our kids an antiquated clunker phone?

No.

I usually recommend teenagers have a mobile plan that provides somewhere between 1GB and 5GB per month. I want you to march into your telco provider with a script and say this:

You: 'Hello, delightful staff, we need to review our family mobile phone package. We want our children to have a plan with unlimited calls and texts, but only 2 to 5GB of data per month.'

Them: 'Just to make sure you don't get stung with bill-shock, we'll activate your family sharing so when one of you runs out it will automatically use another family member's data allowance.'

You: 'Thank you for your concern, but that's a hard no from me. **I don't want family sharing because my kids will use 95 per cent of our data.** I want a plan that caps their data and when they run out, they have to wait until the next month to get more. You see, I think they'll learn how to manage their usage better that way.'

Them: 'Would you like this promotional deal that allows free data on certain social media apps or streaming services? It's an amazing offer!'

You: 'No, I don't want any of that.'

Them: 'Well our base plan comes with 20GB of data. We don't have a plan that offers less. Would you like that one?'

You: '**No, the Unplugged Pysch will yell at me and my kid won't go to bed on time.** I'll shop around and find someone who has the plan I described.'

Are there any other solutions?

Some of the tech products I mentioned in Unplugged Step 1 (pages 140–7) do have features to manage mobile phone use. In theory, you're able to block access from a smartphone to its own data.

In my experience, both at the clinic and when speaking with some of these companies, **these features are not robust and teenagers have found ways around them.** I understand some of these companies are working on possible solutions, but we'll have to watch this space.

There are, however, some smartphone apps that have rolled out in the last year or two that could be helpful. They allow more specific parent controls on mobile phones.

If your child uses an Apple iPhone, then the Screen Time app could be what you're looking for.

I was sceptical when I first started using it, but I've been pleasantly surprised. **Screen Time allows you to set limits on certain apps or lock down a phone's features at certain times.**

There are a few flaws when using the Screen Time app with children and teens, so follow these key set-up steps:

1 **Take the time to actually understand how it works before implementing it.** Test it on your own phone for a week before you try to roll it out with the kids. **Don't assume you've put on an iron-clad password because, in reality, kids can find a way around it quickly.** That may be through your poor choice of password, or you not setting it up correctly so that password covers all features. As a side note, don't type the password in while they are watching and then be surprised as to how they broke your rules. It happens more often than we think when we're living busy lives and reaching for the screen to placate our kids.

2 **Avoid setting specific time limits,** such as limiting social media to 30 minutes per day. In my experience, kids get around this with ease. **Instead, use it to disable all features apart from the basic ones like phone calls, alarms and music between certain hours.** If your child goes to bed at 9 pm, you could set up their phone to become incredibly boring between 8.30 pm and 7 am (or whatever time they need to wake up).

One of the most common debates I hear in my clinic goes like this:

Teen: 'My parents are out of control, man. They try to take my phone at night!'

Parent: 'You shouldn't need a phone then – you're supposed to be sleeping.'

Teen: 'I don't even look at it! I just need it to set an alarm so I wake up in the morning and to listen to music to get to sleep.'

Parent: 'I bought you a clock radio, just use that?'

Teen: 'As if! That's so ancient! See what I'm dealing with, mate?'

This is where in-built screen restrictions can help you break the deadlock. **Set up the password and have all the fun stuff turn off at bedtime.**

Your take-home message

Use apps like Screen Time as an add-on or supplementary strategy to your overall Unplugged plan.

They should NOT be the only thing you use.

Remember: Your best course of action is to find a mobile phone plan that gives your child very limited data, so you can control the Wi-Fi.

Internet on, internet off.

TRY THIS QUICK EXPERIMENT

Do you find yourself a slave to work emails?

Social media or messaging apps?

Or any other 'bing' your phone makes?

This experiment is for any parent who is subconsciously drawn to look at their phone. Yes, that's you.

If you have an iPhone, set your Screen Time app to turn off all work and social media apps at a reasonable time. For me, it's around 8 pm. That gives me enough time to wrap up any small tasks after my daughter goes to bed, and then unwind with my wife before we nod off.

Remember: <u>sleep is sacred.</u>

And that's not just for children, that's for us big kids as well.

If you find yourself enjoying your unplugged time, why not expand Screen Time controls to other parts of the day?

On the other hand, if you can't stop breaking your own self-imposed limits by putting in your pin code, perhaps ask your partner or friend to set the passcode and remove the temptation.

TIME I SET SCREEN TIME TO TURN OFF:

HOW I'M FINDING IT:

UNPLUGGED STEP 7:

Lock It In

You've arrived at the last major step.

Have you ever negotiated a major purchase like a home?
Or perhaps negotiated a new job with a bumper salary
package? I bet you didn't strut into your current boss's
office and hand in your resignation without having that
new job offer in writing. If you did, you're either very
brave or extremely silly.

**Negotiating the details in person is one thing;
seeing the finer details in black and white is
entirely different.** What if your new boss slipped in
something about working every Christmas Day until the
end of time, and you missed that part of the conversation
that was taking place in the busy café while trying to
politely nod and not ruin this huge opportunity?

This is **not** the part where I tell you I've developed some
whiz-bang Tech Diet contract template you can download
for an additional fee *after* the purchase of this book.

The irony is, all money aside, many parents would prefer to be spoon-fed that contract and fill it in with their teenager. It's less work and replicates the bureaucratic forms we all hate but are trained to complete.

I'll tell you what happens if you pull out any template forms during this negotiation – you'll lose your teenager, instantly. They typically interpret that as a set-up.

> **You**: 'Great, now that we have a deal, let's just write it down (pulling out the form) to make sure you stick to what you said.'
>
> **Teen**: 'What the hell is that? Did you have your lawyer write that? This was a set-up! You started this conversation so casually and then you pull that out of your back pocket?!'
>
> **You**: 'No, no, it's not a legal thing. This Unplugged guy says it helps if we lock in everything we talked about.'
>
> **Teen**: 'Well, he can go shove his plug where the sun don't shine. What a set-up. I didn't want that deal anyway. I like it the way it is now. I'm old enough to make my own decisions.'

Okay, so he's saying we don't write it down. Easy!

No. It has to be written down and locked in.

If you've been vaguely conscious during this book, you'll know my thoughts on children and teenagers trying to argue any grey space, unclear terms and everything in between at any chance they get.

How do you do it?

I alluded to this in the earlier steps. In my office, I use a giant whiteboard, but you can use paper or whatever you have handy.

It should feel more like a brainstorming session than a legal meeting. Let me clarify that.

> YOU want to end up with a legal document scribbled on the board in terminology that's very objective.

> It's either done or it's not. It's either that time or it's not.

> The trick is to keep it casual enough that your child doesn't feel they're being set up.

Once you have an agreement, take a photo on your smartphone or tablet (see, I knew they were good for something!) **and then text or email it to your teenager.**

It's a record of everyone agreeing and is far better than putting that piece of paper on the fridge for your child to rip down during the first meltdown.

Again, do this in a casual way. Something like this:

> **You**: 'Hey, Mike, I'm going to take a quick picture of that, and I'll send it to you and Dad so we all remember. That way you can remind Dad of what Wi-Fi time you're allowed so he doesn't short-change you.'

Don't write lengthy notes on your phone or palm cards and pull them out halfway through making the plan. This is not a business meeting.

That's a quick-fire way to ensure your child goes from healthy negotiation to 'the world is against me'.

Get your game face on

If you don't feel confident that you'll be able to stay on track, complete this *Get Your Game Face On worksheet* as a first step.

Just to be super clear, this is for the parents to complete. Not your child.

Instructions

Write in your preferred answer for each of the first four questions, then go back and put in brackets your bottom line. The point you will just not be able to live with if it goes past that.

For example, if your ideal bedtime is 9 pm on a school night, but you could live with it being 9.30 pm, that's your bottom line. If you agree to 10.30 pm you'll have steam coming out of your ears and it just won't sit right as a parent.

Don't agree to anything that's fundamentally past your bottom line.

Get Your Game Face On worksheet

1. How many hours would we ideally like our child to be online during a school night?

Preferred answer: _____ [Bottom line: _____]

2. What is the ideal bedtime on a school night?

Preferred answer: _____ [Bottom line: _____]

3. How many hours would we ideally like our child to be online during a weekend?

Preferred answer: _____ [Bottom line: _____]

4. What is the ideal bedtime on a weekend?

Preferred answer: _____ [Bottom line: _____]

5. What's our price? What are the three things we would like to see improve?

   1. _____

   2. _____

   3. _____

   (Remember to write tangible behaviours, not just 'respect' or 'better attitude'.)

If you and your partner fundamentally disagree with each other's views on these answers, don't proceed.

> You both need time to think it over and get on the same page.

> You should not even attempt to discuss this with a teenager if you can't come to an agreement first. (Kids have a field day at the negotiating table with two parents who can't agree with each other.)

How long should a contract last?

> Until they're 18 years old?

> Or have repaid me all the money they owe?

The time frame should be clearly written on the plan.

If you get this part right, it can be your best friend.

Get it wrong and it's your worst enemy. If it's too short a period, you'll be worn down by the endless re-negotiating. Too long and you may have locked yourself into an element that's clearly not working.

A typical plan negotiated in my office will run for a school term.

Depending on when the plan is made, that will likely be somewhere between 1 and 3 months. I do this for a few reasons:

1 **It's easier for teenagers to agree to something that's seen as a trial.** Now, if it's successful, you'll push hard and perhaps pull rank to implement it in the longer term, citing all the great ways it has helped.

2 **If it's not successful, it gives an opportunity for your teenager to feel heard again, and an opportunity for you to tweak the rules.**

3 **The most important reason to have time-limited reviews is that most kids will insist on some smaller points that you know full well are not going to work.** If this becomes an impasse at the negotiation phase, you may choose to agree to that part for a short period, and if they can't manage that, it will be changed in the next plan.

The most concrete example I can give you is convincing teenage boys they need tutoring.

Often, parents will come to me with solid results such as, 'he has literally failed the last three maths tests', or with feedback from the teacher that he is falling behind.

Telling a teenager they MUST go to tutoring rarely has them skipping along, maths book in hand.

Instead, I usually ask the teenager what their plan is to improve in that area. They'll give me some vague rhetoric like, 'I just need to work harder. I don't need a tutor. I can do the work myself every Saturday.'

I then encourage parents to negotiate a period for the teenager to try their plan and set a goal for the next test. If they don't reach that goal, we tell the teen that will then result in trying Mum and Dad's plan of hiring a tutor once a week.

We all know the teenager's vague plan is unlikely to work.

But the longer we argue that in theory the more conflict we create.

In most circumstances, it's easier to put deadlines and boundaries around that plan and have them test it out. **They're usually much more willing to try the alternate plan if they feel they had a crack at their own first.**

One thing is crystal clear.

Parents must honour the contract or plan just as we are expecting a child or teenager to do.

There can be no room for double standards.

Yes, you're the parents and shouldn't feel this is a straightforward democracy, but you should only pull rank if it's absolutely necessary.

You see, pulling rank only works so many times before you have a full-blown rebellion on your hands. Best to save it for special occasions.

You need a starting point, even if it's not perfect

In general, I encourage parents to concede some small parts when negotiating and locking in a plan.

I've negotiated plans in my office where we've agreed on 90 per cent of things, but the teenager wants a 10.30 pm bedtime (Wi-Fi off) and the parents demand 10 pm. In many cases, the teenager has already bargained and been flexible on many elements but refuses to give this up.

Now, if this hypothetical teen had to get up at 5.30 am every morning to make it to school, I can understand the parents won't accept a plan that has a maximum of 7 hours sleep total.

But in reality, if he has to be awake at 7 am, we are talking about the difference between 8.5 and 9 hours sleep.

Is it really worth sabotaging the entire deal for that?

> **If you have the major things covered and you find yourself bending on some small things, that's better than having no deal at all.**

This is precisely why the *Get Your Game Face On worksheet* asks you about your ideal numbers, and then your bottom line.

It's a starting point.

You're able to build in logical markers from there.

In the example above, if the reason you're not keen to budge on bedtime is because your teen has a pattern of getting to school late, you may elect to accept their later bedtime request on the proviso they get to school on time every day.

<u>Set up a clear goal as a side note to the plan.</u>
It looks something like this:

10.30 pm bedtime (Wi-Fi off) but will be reviewed at end of school term. If school records indicate late more than three times this year, it will revert to 10 pm next term.

Anytime you can link a goal or behaviour to something that's judged by an external person, it limits the need for conflict in the family.

Think of it as outsourcing.

Why argue with your teenager about whether they were late to school that day or if a magical unicorn got them there in record time when you can simply ask for the school record at the end of the term?

What about school holidays?

The dreaded school holidays. **In general, I agree with children and teenagers who argue, 'It's my holiday, I should get more time.'** Within reason.

If they're getting 2 hours of internet time on a school night, you might feel 4 or 5 hours is appropriate during the school holidays.

Of course, it's easier to come up with a holiday plan if you have an existing plan in place for school days.

It allows for a logical starting point.

When negotiating a school holiday plan, consider the general balance.

If they have a week away camping, you may validate and agree to an extra hour per day for the week they're back.

Use commonsense and, when that fails or you're questioning your gut, go back to the five developmental domains in Chapter 5: When Should Parents Panic? and look at the school holidays as a bigger picture.

Ask yourself if they're meeting most of those areas with this plan before you sign off on it.

This is yet another example of why, in my opinion, <u>guidelines for 'how many hours' per day or week are grossly misleading.</u>

Two teenagers may both negotiate 5 hours per day screen time with their parents during the holidays.

Teenager One spends their other 19 hours like this:

> 9 hours of sleep

> 1 hour studying

> 4 hours working at their part-time job

> 5 hours working up a sweat surfing at the beach with mates

It would be hard to argue that's not a healthy balance.

Teenager Two spends their other 19 hours like this:

> 10 hours of sleep (but from 2 am till 12 noon)

> 4 hours on their phone around the house

> 1 hour teasing younger brother due to general boredom

> 4 hours in their bedroom with the door closed

Two teens. Same total hours of screen or Wi-Fi time. **Two completely different outcomes.**

The Tech Diet summary

In this chapter, we've gone through the major steps in applying a Tech Diet for teenagers. Here are the four core things you need to do for any successful plan:

1 **Take control of the Wi-Fi: <u>internet on, internet off.</u>**

2 **Reframe the Wi-Fi as a reward, not a right.**

3 **Negotiate a plan and name your price** (the behaviour you want to see from them).

4 **Don't let their access to mobile data undermine your plan.**

Get the calendar out! Let's go through for how long and when to implement each Unplugged Step.

CHAPTER 7

THE
TECH DIET
TIMELINE

Week-by-week Tech Diet timeline

WEEK 1
- Both parents read this book (or at the very least the Unplugged Steps)
- Complete the Chapter 5 *Should I Panic?* parent checklist
- Get on the same page with the Chapter 6 *Get Your Game Face On worksheet*

WEEK 2
- Follow Unplugged Steps 1 and 2
- Decide what tech solutions or upgrades you need to assist you in implementing the plan at home. If you're not confident, it's time to call your IT expert

WEEKS 3–4
- Follow Unplugged Steps 3–7
- Negotiate a schedule

WEEKS 5–10
- Monitor the plan and troubleshoot when needed

LAST WEEK OF SCHOOL TERM
- Negotiate a new schedule for the school holidays

SCHOOL HOLIDAYS
- Implement school holiday schedule from Day 1

I find the Unplugged Steps and the associated troubleshooting to be most effective when applied over a school term and a connecting school holiday period.

In an ideal world, you'll have 10 weeks of a school term and 2 weeks of the school holidays to really nail it.

Of course, this is an ideal timeline that should have your child's Tech Diet back in balance in one school term.

In reality, some of the steps may take you a shorter or longer time.

Some parents spend 1 week troubleshooting and don't need the full 5 weeks allowed. Others find that while things are improving, they still need to do some minor troubleshooting in the holidays or next school term.

Overall, there's wiggle room in this timeline.

Don't freak out if you're not following it to the letter. It should be used as a guide to ensure you keep moving at a healthy pace and don't lose steam.

If you're reading this book and it's already midway through the school term ...

Don't throw your hands in the air and wait 2 months for the next school term to start.

I advise you to jump in at the next logical point, which will likely be starting with the school holidays plan.

If you did attempt to get started mid-term, it would likely result in a rushed version of this timeline and skipping important details.

In general, most families need a solid 4 to 5 weeks to implement a plan during a school term.

So, if it's Week 8 already, there's probably not enough time for you to get this in place before the end of the term.

Bottom line

I strongly suggest you don't rush your timeline.

After reading the broader Unplugged Steps, some of you may feel like we haven't covered all the small nagging questions along the way.

Ultimately, it's all about getting your child to buy in.

CHAPTER 8

GETTING YOUR TEENAGER TO DRINK THE KOOL-AID

You're not a super-parent. Be realistic. Keep it simple.

It's not uncommon to have parents come in to my clinic having tried multiple screen plans before seeing me.

> **The biggest mistake we make as parents is trying to implement an overly complicated plan.**

'Every second Thursday he goes to karate, so he's allowed 27 minutes of gaming when we get home, but every other Thursday it's 46 minutes.'

Incredible!

How on earth do you time that? I struggle to keep track of my toast getting burnt in the morning let alone a plan with odd times and days.

In this chapter, I'll take you through the common questions I get asked in my clinic and at my parent talks. After hearing from thousands of families, I feel it's a comprehensive sample of what the average Australian family faces at home.

We've already discussed the tech software that can help with this. But ultimately, **the simpler the plan the more likely you will be able to keep it straight in your head and know if your teenager has found a way around it.**

This also includes parents who agree to specific demands made by their children.

> **Teen:** 'I'll go to tutoring, but you better have me home for my 5 pm screen time.'

Then, of course, the session runs late or your other child eats too many donuts in the car and decides to have a cheeky spew ... You know, all the standard life stuff.

Acknowledge that your teen has missed some of their time and adjust, but don't apologise for honest life events getting in the way. **If you feel like you have a mini dictator barking orders, something is off.**

Why can't my child see this is best for them?

Don't get stuck arguing the value of gaming or screen time. You can't win that fight.

There will be no light-bulb moment where your child says, 'Hey, Dad, you know after quoting me all this research, I can see your argument has more merit than mine. Let's make a plan!'

In my experience, teenagers will fall into one of three categories:

1 **Teenagers who agree it's best for them and are willing to follow the rules with minimal complaint.** If your child is in this category, congratulations on your lottery win, but probably best not to brag too much to other parents.

2 **Teenagers who agree in principle that a healthy Tech Diet is important but break the rules at every opportunity.** Try not to get too carried away feeling this is some kind of personal assault on your parenting. It's simply a teenager caving to temptation. Calmly apply the consequences as per the plan and move on.

3 **Those who don't agree there should be any moderation in use, refuse to engage in it and fight it all the way.** Strap yourself in, it's going to get bumpy. For these teenagers, there's not much to be gained debating the pros and cons of healthy use. Embrace the fact you're viewed as 'the world's worst parent' for applying rules and you're not there to be your child's best mate. That's not your job. That comes later in life when they mature and have some ability to thank you for guiding them.

Every time we even talk about gaming or screen time it gets heated.

Accept that, as an ancient tech dinosaur, you don't understand your child's view. Even if you're a hip parent who games with your kids, you're still a dinosaur in their eyes.

In my experience, **it's worthwhile taking the time to actually understand the games, apps or social media your child uses.**

Ask yourself: why is my child so infatuated with this? And be enthusiastic – or at least try and fake enthusiasm – when your child is showing you how it works.

If you have older teenagers, you may have missed the boat with this. Your request will likely be met with grunts, groans and if you're lucky, a single 'no'. Don't be discouraged, you may find an opening one day when they're in a decent mood.

Why do I suggest this?

What happens if you pull the plug or demand your child leaves a game early? You're probably recalling the anger outbursts that come from this, but seriously, do you know what happens in the game?

> **Depending on the specific game, there are various consequences for leaving early.**

This can range from penalties or experience points being deducted all the way through to being locked out of the game for a period. That's right. **Some games freeze or lock your account for something that's seen as treason.**

Consider this: if your child is playing a game that all their friends play and has just been locked out for a week, that's as good as being socially excluded or shunned.

If you understand broadly how the game works, it will help you when implementing your Tech Diet.

For example, if a game takes on average 30 to 40 minutes to play and you're offering your child a 30-minute block of free internet time, that's going to be a big NO DEAL on their end.

In saying this, I don't want you to get into a never-ending debate about what they want to do and why you're ancient and couldn't possibly understand. This typically escalates and leads nowhere good.

If you find yourself in a circular debate with teenage logic being a feature, just bow out.

Use humour if that's in your wheelhouse: 'I have no idea 'cause I'm like 300 years old and was born in the industrial revolution,' and walk away.

Shouldn't my child take ownership and learn how to manage screen time without me?

This is a great question I get asked often. **What a utopia that would be!**

The best way I can explain this is by referencing what I do when giving student workshops on a healthy Tech Diet. The majority of high school students can accept (between throwing pieces of fruit at me on stage) that there is a healthy limit to how much sugar we should all consume per day.

Depending on what data you look at, it's something in the region of 6 to 9 teaspoons per day.[4] The average Australian consumes somewhere in the region of 22 to 27 teaspoons per day. We're all aware that sugar is lurking in many wonderful products, including a range of delicious fruit drinks and soft drinks.

My question to you: would you stock your kitchen up with every type of food and drink containing high-sugar content and let your children eat whatever and whenever they like?

I'll assume you answered no.

It's a small proportion of children who'd be able to resist the temptation of that sugar and stick to the recommended amount. I see parallels with children's screen time.

It's important we set boundaries and limits and hope when they're adults that they figure out a healthy balance themselves. Hopefully sooner rather than later.

We had a deal that my child would do their homework if they could have screen time first. Then they refused to get off!

The old 'pay me before I've done my end of the deal' trick. I know you're desperate to believe that your teenager will hold up their end of the bargain, but there must be some part of you that knows taking the easy road and caving to their terms will end in tears. For you that is.

It's pretty simple and comes back to the earlier section in the very first Unplugged Step: **frame the internet as a reward, not a right.**

Commonsense suggests if you give a kid the reward before they do what you've asked, you're rolling the dice. Roll away if you choose, but don't be surprised if it ends badly.

Bottom line

Collect your end of the bargain first, then pay out the screen time. Don't try it the other way around.

My child wants to earn bonus screen time. That's a good life lesson, right?

This is a tough one. And it's not black and white.

In the scenario where your child has lost all their internet time due to poor behaviour or refusing to do what you asked – breaking the rules you negotiated – then I don't recommend allowing them to redeem themselves, even if they're willing to wash your car or vacuum the house.

> **It's important for them to learn there are consequences to their choices.**

This is one of the reasons I recommend the 'maximum penalty: 24 hours' rule.

The exception is on weekends and school holidays when there's more time in the day. If you as parents feel the plan has minimal internet allowance for their age, you may wish to offer a one-off bonus 30 or 60 minutes for doing something you think contributes to their overall wellbeing. It might be exercise, extra tutoring if they're behind academically or some much-needed family time.

All said, you need to be mindful it doesn't turn into a never-ending nag marathon with your children wearing you down seeking bonus time.

If you end up in this position, put a clear stop to all bonus time negotiations for a set period.

Draw a line in the sand to ensure you don't have a moment of weakness.

I read an article about the benefits of technology for children. Is that true?

Absolutely. There are benefits to internet, screen and gaming time.

One Australian study reported gaming can improve overall wellbeing through relaxation, stress management, social relationships, sense of accomplishment and mastery.[5] It's one of the reasons I don't recommend the cold turkey approach.

Kids with no access to the internet receive none of the wellbeing benefits.

But there's a catch.

Most wellbeing studies find that this is true for those with a *healthy* balance or Tech Diet.

Excessive use is found to have negative impacts on your overall wellbeing.

For divorced or separated parents

Okay, time for some commonsense:

> **In an ideal world, divorced or separated parents who are co-parenting would both follow the Tech Diet and each Unplugged Step and sit down together with their children to negotiate a plan that will be respected at both houses.** In reality, and for myriad reasons I don't care to go into, this can be difficult for some divorced or separated parents to do.

> **The next best thing would be for one parent who has read or heard of the Unplugged Steps to suggest both parents read the book. If they both vaguely agree this is something they would like to do, they can each negotiate a plan for their respective households.** Of course, this is riddled with landmines as one parent will naturally be more lenient than the other and hence your child or teenager will use that to complain endlessly. So be prepared and confident when this occurs and stick with your gut.

While it's not ideal to have two separate plans over two houses, if you're both following the same Unplugged philosophy your plans will have the same fundamental features, which is important.

> **As a last resort, if one parent is flat-out refusing and fundamentally disagrees with my method, but you feel differently, there's nothing stopping you from applying the Tech Diet in just your house** and accepting it will be a watered-down version, as you have no control over what happens when they're at their other parent's house. The other person is free to parent however they see fit, I'm not here to jump up and down about it.

Should I let my child play unlimited educational games?

They're learning – what could be wrong with that?

I'm not all that concerned about the benefits of educational games versus those for entertainment. I think this is largely a parent's choice.

What I will say is any game or app should not be used to excess.

I don't care if it's helping them be an advanced maths student. Two reasons why I say this:

1 **Anything in excess means we're not getting balance.** Remember: it's important for a child to develop in all areas. I hold the same view about excessive tutoring for children. It has its place, but at the extreme end it's taking away hours in their day from other activities like sport, family time or just having fun.

2 **The unlimited educational games policy may be followed by younger children.** But one day you'll leave them on that spelling app and return to them playing a game or watching YouTube. **This is the start of a never-ending debate around what is educational.**

(I once told my mum playing SimCity 2000 on the family PC was educational. You know, it's helping me follow my dream of being a town planner ... She didn't buy it. Ran a pretty tight ship my mum did.)

When I take the internet away my child says they don't care, they'll just watch TV or play offline.

Classic bluff.

I've seen teenagers calmly follow through with this strategy for days. (I'm sure they have a future at the World Series of Poker.)

Offline gaming and TV have been around since I was a kid. I think I turned out okay? It's entertaining, I could spend a few hours at a time playing FIFA Soccer 96.

The point I'm making is that those games were offline.

In my experience, there is a hierarchy or pyramid that most children find more fun. It goes a little something like this:

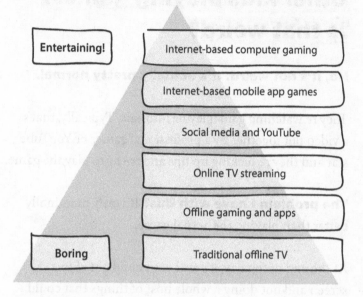

- Entertaining!
  - Internet-based computer gaming
  - Internet-based mobile app games
  - Social media and YouTube
  - Online TV streaming
  - Offline gaming and apps
- Boring
  - Traditional offline TV

> By removing the internet access, you're cutting access to the top four on that pyramid.

> Removing the bottom two would involve you pulling the flat screen off the wall and physically prising the console or device from their hand.

As we've said before, this may escalate things in the house and for little impact. **There is only so much daytime TV and offline gaming a teenager can endure before caving and ending their sit-in.**

When I ban gaming my child watches videos of other kids playing games. Is that weird?

No, it's not weird. It's actually pretty normal.

They're watching gameplay or tutorials. Typically, that's a video put together by a professional gamer or YouTube star and they're picking up tips and tricks to play the game.

The problem I have with this? It's only marginally better than playing the actual game.

At the end of the day, it's still your child glued to a screen and not doing a whole host of things that could contribute to a well-rounded little human.

It's one of the primary reasons behind my **internet on, internet off** rule.

When parents ban specific games or activities online, kids will usually just head down the pyramid and find the next best thing.

My kid wants to be a pro-gamer when he grows up ... is that even a thing?

This is a real doozy. There are largely two categories of pro your child may be dreaming of:

1 **Pro-gamers**

2 **YouTuber stars and social media influencers**

Pro-gamers

Pro-gaming is lucrative.

The top people in the world make some serious money. So don't dismiss your child or scoff at this suggestion, it's true. **The dilemma is the sacrifices made to get to that level.**

It's not uncommon to hear that pro-gamers have quit school around age 10 or 12 to join a team and train full-time.

The best analogy I can use is a sporting one. If your child told you they wanted to quit school to be a professional rugby player, our culture as Australians encourages kids to dream big and shoot for the stars. So you might tell them they need to finish school as a back-up plan but encourage their training as a professional. That's where the analogy ends – I didn't say it was a good one.

Are you then going to allow your child to game every waking moment outside of school? Perhaps not such a great idea.

The reason I use that analogy is because that's how most children or teenagers see it. That's their perspective. For them, the plan is no different from their brother telling you he wants to be the world's best footballer (Tim Cahill, for the record).

There's not a step-by-step answer or 'how to' list to solve this one if it crops up.

But you're halfway there if you acknowledge that's a reasonable ambition in their mind and proceed with a calm but commonsense reply.

YouTube stars and social media influencers

In my opinion, aspiring YouTube stars and social media influencers are slightly less tricky to deal with. It's not something that requires 14 hours a day on a screen, although I'm sure many of the successful ones put in a shift like that.

If you feel it's safe for your child or teenager to pursue that dream, then put in place appropriate boundaries around internet use – as we discussed in the Unplugged Steps – and let them figure it out for themselves.

When I say 'safe', I'm talking about cyber-safety.

You need to ensure the topic or interest that your child's social media or YouTube account will feature:

✓ **is age appropriate**
✓ **won't attract unsavoury attention**

Bottom line

If you go down the path of 'No, I won't allow it, it's a complete waste of time and will never eventuate', **you're inviting them to dig their heels in and prove you wrong.**

No double jeopardy rule

Parents often tell me their child got in trouble at school, was punished, then they added on a technology or screen ban for a few weeks for good measure. Just to really drive the point home.

This is again a personal parenting decision.

I recommend a 'no double jeopardy' rule, meaning if they've already been punished at school, they shouldn't be punished at home.

The classic example goes a little something like this:

Me: 'What happened at school?'

Teen: 'I didn't hand in my homework. That teacher never checks! I thought I would get away with it. What a jerk. He was on a power trip and gave me an afternoon detention.'

Me: 'So what did you do?'

Teen: 'Well, I wasn't happy, but I did the detention. Copped it sweet. And then I get home and Dad lost it and banned all screens for a week! What's that about? So, I went off!'

Classic double jeopardy. **If the school has taken care of it, why bother entering into that conflict?**

I'm not suggesting you should be doing high-fives with your child for getting in trouble. A simple, 'Well, you did the wrong thing, you got caught, you did the detention. Let's move on,' is usually enough.

Why? Because you should save your fire-power and energy for any breaking of rules at home or outside of school. It's as simple as that.

Why be the bad guy in a situation when the teachers have taken care of it?

There is one main exception to the no double jeopardy rule: **if your child or teenager has been suspended, they should not be allowed internet access during that time.**

If they are, it's almost seen as a reward to some kids. Get suspended, get yelled at for a while, then get a few days of relaxing and gaming!

In that scenario, you should fall back on the rule of **'no school = no internet'.** That includes suspensions.

232 The Tech Diet for Your Child & Teen

Should we be setting a better example as parents?

Yes and no.

This is what I call a hand-grenade question.
A classic asked at one of my talks that's usually drawing me into an ongoing argument, or in polite terms, a 'difference of opinion' that two parents are having on the topic.

The idea that our children model our behaviour and the example we set is not ground-breaking – it's been around for a while. If you have a family rule that there should be no devices, screens or phones at the dinner table – an actual personal favourite of mine – then it's hard to enforce if you as parents don't adhere to it.

However, if you implement a rule about screens and internet going off at 9 pm in order to get your child to bed, **I don't think you should be lectured by your offspring if that rule doesn't apply to you.**

Some context:

I would ask you as a parent to reflect on the purpose of your screen time. Are you at times mindlessly flicking through the overnight highlights from Liverpool FC's latest derby win over Manchester United when you really should be playing tea parties with your daughter?

Guilty.

Shock, horror, the Unplugged Psychologist is human!

But, at times, parents have to meet work or family demands that require the use of their screens.

Love it or hate it, that's the modern-day workforce.

I'm not here to lecture parents; sometimes, you need to do what you need to do.

I read about how going off-grid probably won't help, but what if I send my kid on one of those bush camps?

I know this is tempting. What's not to like about it?

You send your kid into the bush with some full-on Bear Grylls character and they come back with zero need for screens and the ability to start a campfire using only three eucalyptus leaves, some bark and good vibes.

On top of that, you get a whole week of blissful peace, 8 hours sleep and maybe even an uninterrupted date night. Brilliant! Money well spent.

If you've been paying attention up until now you'll know my thoughts on going cold turkey: it doesn't work.

Do I think the bush survival skills would be a nice change for your teenager? Yeah, for sure.

Will it change any of their tech habits when they return? Slim to no chance.

What I feel does work are camps where they pair the activities, outdoors and Bear Grylls stuff with education about healthy gaming and negotiating a plan with the parents before returning home.

That would be amazing.

If we could do the Unplugged Steps in a camp or bush setting like that it would likely take the sting out of some of the reaction and help bring them to the table.

I'm yet to find that program in Australia, but that doesn't mean it's not out there. I did recently consider starting a program like this before my wife reminded me that I wear far too many hats without starting my own bush camp.

Plus, I don't own a bush camp. Minor flaw in my plan … I may consider running the therapy part in future should there be a Bear Grylls out there able to run the rest?

You've followed the plan but feel like it's not working?

Let's troubleshoot together.

CHAPTER 9

RECIPE FOR DISASTER: WHEN IT ALL GOES PEAR-SHAPED

Troubleshooting

So, you've ...

✓ Done your research

✓ Had a long hard think about how your child is tracking in the five developmental domains

✓ Implemented all (or some) of the Unplugged Steps

✓ And you're still struggling ...

First thing to consider: have you implemented a watered-down version of the Unplugged Steps in the Tech Diet?

If so, you may have underestimated your child's ability to dig in for a battle and **you may need to consider tightening the boundaries.**

If that's not the case, then this section is for troubleshooting.

When I first implement a new plan with families in my clinic, they ask me when they should book our next appointment. I always respond with something like, '**Don't leave it too long.** You need to come back and tell me all the ways your lovely child has pushed or broken the rules so we can troubleshoot.'

I'm not being negative about the plan; I'm simply sending them two important take-home messages:

1 **No plan is perfect.**
No plan is one size fits all.
There will be hiccups in the first few weeks and even months.

2 **Don't get discouraged – it's normal.**
We just regroup and troubleshoot together. Most of the troubleshooting questions parents and families return with are stock standard. But every now and then I get thrown a new one just to keep me on my toes.

If you're struggling with any of the following problems, it may be time to consider expert help from a health professional.

When things turn aggressive

Violence or physical aggression is not okay in any household and in any form.

That most certainly includes parents being physically aggressive with children, but it also includes the reverse.

The Tech Diet is geared towards trying to take the heat out of physically taking devices, while at the same time not passively standing by while your kid calls the shots. However, unfortunately, I still see aggression and violence as a regular reaction to limits being set.

Let's set one thing straight: if you feel there's aggression to the point of feeling concerned for the safety of yourself or anyone else in the home, you should call the police.

I'm not suggesting they'll take your child away in handcuffs or give them a stern talking to. The truth is, no one knows what action the police will take, but they're professionals trained to assess the situation and make decisions to keep people safe.

I can appreciate that's a difficult thing for parents to do.

Sometimes it takes parents two or three incidents before they follow that advice.

In my experience, **if a child or teenager uses physical aggression to get the family to back down and it results in them getting what they want (= more screen time) they're likely to use it again.**

Calling the police in these situations can help shift this behaviour.

It is, in some circumstances, enough of a consequence to have your teenager rethink that strategy.

The other resource is a pre-emptive one.

Police stations in NSW have designated **Youth Liaison and School Liaison officers who are specifically trained in helping children get back on track.** You can contact your local station to get in touch with them. I'm sure there are the same or similar services in other states.

Teenagers are sometimes dismissive and deny they've ever been aggressive, claiming they 'don't remember that'. This is usually a way of avoiding an embarrassing topic in which they know their behaviour is out of line or even illegal.

More commonly, teenagers will admit they became aggressive and are remorseful about it. They have every intention in that moment, when calm, to never repeat it.

It's important that we stay calm and safe in response to any aggression. And when things have settled down, follow the Tech Diet and implement the consequence of reduced internet access.

If your teenager is breaking things and getting verbally aggressive ...

Well, that escalated quickly. It's best to stay calm and only step in if you feel they're in an unsafe situation.

What's this unsafe situation stuff? You sound like a politician, mate! Fair call, here's a clear and plain example:

> > If your child is angry and throwing a book against a wall or hitting a pillow against a door, I would say that's not ideal but it's unlikely to hurt anyone.
>
> > If your child has picked up the ornamental wooden axe you bought in Bali and is headed towards the glass door, then that's entering the unsafe zone.

Just use your best parent Spidey senses and commonsense on this one.

Refusing to go to school

This is more common than you think. **The old 'you limit my internet and I'm not going to school' threat.** I've had kids threaten this and never follow through. I've also had kids threaten this and dig themselves in to the point of missing entire school terms.

In my experience, you can't exactly predict which path your child will take. In general, the more invested they are in the internet and the longer this has been going on unchecked, the more likely they are to dig themselves a trench and hunker down.

I recommend that parents don't negotiate with these threats. Ever. It does not end well.

That also means you need to be willing to wait it out like a good old-fashioned sit-in.

You'll calmly, but firmly, explain that if they choose not to go to school, there's nothing you can do to physically drag them there, but **they'll have zero internet access until they go.** If you're in this territory, you need to implement every single one of the Unplugged Steps and do it damn well.

At this point, you should double-check with school staff that there is no other reason your child is avoiding school. If they've been bullied, had a fight with friends or are behind in school work, this can complicate getting them back to school. And this needs to be addressed separately.

Your strategy here is to bore them. Bore them until they agree to return.

Teenagers often look for more attention or interaction during this time. Be short, pleasant and to the point with them, but don't find yourself buying them books or playing a board game with them in order to break up the monotony of not going to school. **The simple answer is all privileges and life as you know it will return the minute you go back to school.**

When they do return to school, they should be rewarded with internet time immediately that evening.

Often, they'll go to school for a few days, then not, then back to school, then not. **Continue with only giving internet access on the days they have attended.**

If they've been away from school for more than a day or two, you'll need to carefully manage their re-entry. Seek the school's support to ensure they're not bombarded with work when they return; this may trigger further school refusal as they may feel 'everyone is against me'.

Is your child gaming the system?

Sometimes, parents return for a troubleshooting session and tell me the measures have had zero impact on their child's behaviour in the first few weeks. Their child is still refusing to do anything the parents ask and they don't care about losing internet time. **They almost smile and look smug when you take time away from them.**

Something is VERY wrong.

Are you trying to tell me your teenager smiled at your consequence, calmly went to their bedroom and shut the door all night?

Did you seriously think they were just doing extra maths homework in there?

I would say you have a 90 per cent chance that the tech solutions you implemented haven't done their job.

Your first play should be changing all the passwords.

Just in case your original password of their middle name and date of birth, which you assumed was uncrackable, has been hacked.

Once you've done this, sit back for a day or so and see if there are any fireworks. You'll know if you fixed the problem – it'll be very apparent next time they leave their room.

If you're still puzzled, it might be worth some tactful and polite spot checks.

This is your good old wander in an hour after bedtime to see if they're asleep or knocking to ask if they want you to bring them a drink.

If they look like they're scrambling with an electronic device when you walk in, you're on the right track.

And if all else fails, it's time to call in the big guns.

Call your local IT expert one day when the entire family is out, explain what you're trying to do and ask them to double-check every setting and system you stumbled your way through. It's often something obvious to them and, if so, it was obvious to your child, too.

Mobile hotspots

A common gap in your high-tech system is the use of mobile hotspots.

We covered this idea in Unplugged Step 6: Minimise Mobile Data. Any phone or device that can be connected to a data plan can be used to tether and hotspot a computer, tablet or other device, granting it internet access.

It's not uncommon for older teenagers who have a part-time job and access to their own savings (or access to any of their parents' accounts), to go out and purchase another device or router.

Tucked strategically under their pillow, or somewhere more creative, **they'll happily use your Wi-Fi when allowed and then switch over to their secret hotspot when it turns off.**

You can see how this provides very little motivation to follow any of your requests.

My child has a job and is using their own money to buy data

Now, that's a pickle!

In this scenario, their job will be taking up two or three evenings or weekends per week, which is automatically a parent win. It's improving multiple areas of development – especially social development – and results in less time available to sit at home on screens.

If they've earned money through working and call up the local internet provider to install their own internet line, that's a hard no from you.

It's your name on the lease or mortgage, so you can politely tell the provider you do not consent.

However, they can still use their money to top up data on mobile devices. If you find yourself in this territory, **it's tricky because it's their money to spend.**

I'd start looking at all the other things you fund as a parent.

Things like their holiday spending, lunch money and any other privilege you currently pay for.

Have a conversation around them having expendable cash from their job to spend on data and your view that they should start paying for other things.

Once they've calmed down after that conversation, suggest they put a portion of their job earnings into a savings account and assure them they can spend it how they like – with the exception of buying endless data or gaming items.

At the end of the day, you're walking a bit of a tight rope.

You don't want them to throw their hands in the air and quit their job.

But at the same time, you can't have them working a minimal amount with the sole purpose of undermining your screen and internet rules.

Gifts and gift cards

'Dear Uncle Steve, please don't buy my kids any gift cards you see in the servo on your way to Christmas dinner. Also, please don't give them cash. I would rather you buy them an ugly sweater they won't wear. Cheers.'

Gift cards and cash can all be used to purchase data or items in a game.

I'm not suggesting you bankrupt your child. If they're working or earning money, then all power to them. Remember, if they're working for money, that's an activity that is building social skills and physically reducing the number of hours possible to spend online.

But you don't need good old Uncle Steve throwing out pineapples on Christmas Day when you've just worked so hard to limit their phone data.

Threatening self-harm

When any child or teenager threatens to harm themselves in any way, it's serious.

I'd be negligent to suggest any strategy or pearls of wisdom I write here will be an appropriate response.

There is only one response: seek immediate assistance from your GP, school counsellor, or appropriate mental health professional.

> **If you have immediate concerns for their safety, you should attend your local Hospital Emergency Department for an urgent mental health assessment.**

One in five children and teenagers are affected by mental illness in Australia.

Healthy screen time is not impossible if your child suffers from mental illness, it just makes things trickier.

CHAPTER 10

OTHER MENTAL HEALTH DISORDERS: WHERE DO THEY FIT IN TO THIS?

If your child doesn't suffer from any other mental health symptoms, feel free to skip this chapter.

If you're worried about your child's mental health in general, it may be useful information to keep in your back pocket.

In any case, if your child does have one of the following or any other diagnosable mental health condition, you should implement the Tech Diet under the supervision of a mental health professional.

In this chapter, I'll outline some of the main mental health disorders that I see are co-morbid with gaming and internet overuse. (Co-morbid being a fancy term for two things that come together.)

This is not an exhaustive list, just my observations on how these mental health conditions can complicate things when implementing a Tech Diet:

> Attention Deficit Hyperactivity Disorder (ADHD)

> Autism Spectrum Disorder (ASD)

> Anxiety

> Depression

The chicken or the egg?

I recently met up with my colleague Dr Philip Tam, a Sydney-based child psychiatrist and fellow expert in the field of all things Gaming Disorder and related.

Often, the conversation turns into the circular debate around **whether problematic levels of gaming or internet use have the ability to 'cause' other mental health disorders.** (I say 'cause' because it's the easiest way to get my point across, but in the research world, proving causation is near impossible.)

Or, is it the other way around? That is, children and teenagers suffering from other mental health disorders or symptoms may end up with higher levels of gaming and internet use.

The old chicken and the egg conundrum.

Neither Philip nor I have a definitive answer on the topic. What we do agree on is the idea that it can probably work both ways. In fact, the process is what Philip calls a 'transactional' model. **One problem makes the other problem worse, which in turn worsens the initial difficulty, causing a downward spiral that is often hard for the clinician to treat.** Many other addictive behaviours, such as problem gambling and alcoholism, follow a similar pattern.

We've both seen families who describe an element of problematic gaming or internet use and other mental health symptoms. I'm not suggesting it's all of them, but it's a high occurrence.

The egg first?

A common example would be a young person who comes to my office with a history of increasing internet or gaming use to the point where it's become unsustainable and it's impacting on the five developmental domains we discussed in Chapter 5.

It's not uncommon for them to develop problems with their mood or, in extreme examples, depressive symptoms if this becomes severe.

Again, some people would call me an alarmist for saying that, but my day-to-day work tells me that's not some crazy idea I've plucked from thin air. Think about it.

I put it to you that anyone – child, teenager or adult – who does an activity that impacts severely on developmental domains like sleep, eating, seeing friends, going to school, etc., is at higher risk of developing depressive symptoms.

Or the chicken?

In some cases, parents and children are able to give me a clear account of a history of other mental health symptoms that occurred first.

For example, if a young person has a history of anxiety and perhaps has had periods of managing those symptoms fairly well but then goes through a period of increased anxiety, they may then start using a game, app or social media as a way of coping with or avoiding those anxious thoughts.

By the time they come to my clinic, the parents may be jumping up and down for me to fix the screen addiction, but that can't be done in isolation or without a comprehensive plan to treat their anxiety.

Attention Deficit Hyperactivity Disorder (ADHD)

I know that ADHD is a controversial topic. Some feel it's over-diagnosed; others feel medication as a primary treatment is over-prescribed. Let's put all that to the side.

Children and teenagers with ADHD are truly amazing gamers.

Gaming plays to their strengths. The bells, sounds, lights, immediate reinforcement – it's almost the complete opposite to sitting in a classroom.

Before all the teachers crucify me for implying that they're boring, hand-on-heart what I'm saying is not a criticism of your teaching. However, in Australia we have an education system that emphasises and rewards a student's ability to concentrate and focus for long periods during exams and assessments. This is every ADHD student's (and parent's) nightmare.

I'm not suggesting we put up our hands and complain the system is rigged, give every ADHD child a leave pass and away we go. But let's think about this through the eyes of a child or teenager.

They're rewarded for their ability and skills in gaming, a domain in which their ADHD is not a crutch, and some would argue is an advantage.

At the same time, they find it hard to get any reward or praise for the traditional tasks at school that require sustained attention and concentration.

In my experience, it makes the online world all the more appealing for ADHD suffers.

Advice to parents of children with ADHD

There's no golden egg I'm trying to lay in this section. The plan remains the same.

I take my hat off to all those parents with a child suffering from ADHD, because your job in managing their Tech Diet is more difficult.

> **There is less room for error and you have to be on top of your game.**

> **For parents of children with ADHD, it's imperative you start young.** I recommend all parents implement the Tech Diet when children are in primary school before it has the chance to snowball.

> **Really emphasise the gaming and internet time as a reward for their efforts in activities that require long periods of attention and concentration.**

Autism Spectrum Disorder (ASD)

I really enjoy working with children and teenagers on the Autism Spectrum. I find them interesting, charming and yes, at times, incredibly frustrating.

When I say ASD, I include high-functioning autism, which was previously categorised as Asperger's. I'm not going to try to describe what ASD is and how to treat it. There are entire books on the topic if you're interested.

The rules of the game are more predictable than the real world.

Children and teenagers with ASD often don't understand the social rules of the real world. It just doesn't come naturally to them. But give them a computer game and the rules are explicit. They are literally written down somewhere and if they're not, some bloke has made a million dollars doing a YouTube channel on it. This is one reason the online world is appealing to those with ASD.

For those of you with some basic knowledge of ASD symptoms, there are a few main areas that become roadblocks to implementing a Tech Diet:

1 **Many – but not all – kids on the spectrum suffer from rigid, or black and white, thinking.** Now, my work colleagues have accused me of being rigid and set in my ways many a time. They often joke I eat the same lunch pretty much every day. Any parent of a child with ASD knows that this is NOT what we're talking about. Rigid thinking for a child on the spectrum is next level. No matter how many ways you try to explain a rule or a concept, it's like pulling teeth. That's just the way their brain works; it's not them trying to be difficult. However, if you find the correct way to explain or justify something it can be a light-bulb moment. Often, the rigidity can then work to your favour as they'll follow the rule religiously. Until you realise there are exceptions to that rule that you did not account for.

2 **The very nature of ASD means they struggle in certain areas around social and communication skills and, in general, reading social cues.** As a side note, the notion that all people on the spectrum don't care about socialising or having friends is incorrect. I meet plenty that yearn to be 'normal' and have a healthy social life.

The method of communication makes it easier to make friends.

The other aspect of gaming, and the internet in general, that makes it appealing to those with ASD is the method of communication. **Most communication is done via chat or text, which takes away many complicated real-life social cues like body language, facial expression and eye contact.** The emergence of video chat and headset communication in gaming doesn't seem to bother kids with ASD. I find they're prone to misreading social cues online at times, but in general, they see it as a much more predictable and safer place to make friends.

Advice to parents of children with ASD

Similar to children with ADHD, **you need to start the Tech Diet younger, and there is less room for error.**

However, there are two key, critical differences:

1 **Kids with ASD will often fundamentally believe that all social needs can be met online.** I've gone down this rabbit hole many times and emerged with zero progress after an hour.

Rigid thinking often makes it difficult to negotiate tech rules in any meaningful way and, at times, you may need to make the decision for them.

2 In my experience, **children with ASD are less likely to care if you remove the internet connection from their games.** That is, online-based games are more attractive to them; however, they're more than content to play offline games. So this may require some tweaking in the Unplugged Steps. **You may need to go down the route of limiting access to physical devices despite me saying this can increase conflict.**

I should mention, I don't think it's an either/or question. **You should still start with the Wi-Fi removal as per the plan, then add in the extra layer of removing devices.** Younger children are far more likely to go along with removing devices, so if you're reading this section because you have a child with ASD, you need to establish a plan in early primary school. If you have a teenager with ASD, it's not too late, but it will be more difficult to put in place.

Anxiety

There are many types of anxiety that can impact children and teenagers. In my view, **the primary type that can occur alongside gaming and internet overuse is social anxiety – the fear of being negatively judged by others.**

This guy can't be serious; he's just described most teenagers! They all freak out about what their friends think of them!

Valid point. And one I usually throw out there myself when I'm talking to parents. It's all about the degree to which a child or teenager is worrying about this. The impact of this can be gauged through the five developmental domains we talked about in Chapter 5, culminating in your *Should I Panic? parent checklist* (see page pages 130–1).

Let's talk real-world examples.

If a teenager already suffers from anxiety, or specifically social anxiety, going to school, sport or any social activity will likely elevate their anxiety.

Kids in general don't have great awareness of what's happening. All they know is, 'I feel better when I don't go, so I stay home.' Often, teenagers won't even give you that much; they just avoid the topic altogether.

In this scenario, I see high rates of reliance on all forms of technology to fill the gap. That is, they can continue to socialise from the 'safety' of their home or bedroom and, as an added bonus, avoid thinking about it at all while they allow themselves to be consumed by technology.

It can also work in reverse. Remember our chicken and egg discussion at the start of this chapter?

Some kids will develop social anxiety symptoms simply due to long periods of isolating themselves while gaming.

Advice to parents of children with anxiety

Without going into the details of treating anxiety, if you have concerns in this area you need to **consult with a mental health professional who can guide you through applying a healthy Tech Diet while at the same time treating underlying anxiety.**

Not something I feel can be done easily by your average family without assistance.

TRY THIS QUICK EXPERIMENT

I challenge you to talk to a parent whose child has spent the majority of a summer holiday (6 to 8 weeks in Australia) at home and online.

Ask them about their child's reaction to going back to school that first week.

It will often range from low-level anxiety or stress about returning to full-blown refusal to get out of bed on day one.

WHO I TALKED TO:

THEIR CHILD'S REACTION TO GOING BACK TO SCHOOL:

Depression

Is gaming making my child depressed?

Frequently, when parents come into my clinic with a child who has an internet or gaming problem, they ask me if their kid is depressed.

Treating young people with depression is complicated. First off, any practitioner who can give you a definitive answer after meeting a child once is kidding themselves. But it's the reason that I routinely do a full mental health screening for any child that walks through the door. **It's another chicken and egg scenario that can start either way.**

Sometimes, I give parents the good news that I don't feel their child has depression or anxiety at that time, despite the concerning screen and tech use.

If we've established that they have a pattern of overuse and their developmental domains are starting to tumble, I'll warn parents their child is at higher risk of developing depression and anxiety symptoms if this pattern continues.

Will it be in 1 week, 1 month or 1 year? Who knows?

Depression is a complex illness with many contributing variables.

If you're told by a professional that your child is at risk of developing depression, as a parent it's probably best to take the steps to change the pattern.

Not really worth rolling the dice while you sit back and see if your child can fix it themselves, right?

Advice to parents of children with depression

Sleep and exercise, on repeat.

I think most mental health professionals agree that a teenager with depression is usually best served starting with a regular sleep pattern and exercise.

The fancy term for this is 'behavioural activation', which is another one of those simple concepts we have jazzed up to sound important. These are not the only steps on the road to treating depression, but they sure are the most practical ones that teenagers and their parents can take on board.

Hopefully, after reading this book you have an appreciation for how often gaming and internet overuse can undermine sleep and exercise.

If you're scratching your head and need a refresher, jump back to Chapter 5: When Should Parents Panic? – it's all there.

CHAPTER 11

FINAL THOUGHTS

Technology to come

Well, this is about the time I exit stage left. But before I do, let's take a look into the future.

I'm often asked about what impact future technology and advancements will have on our children and their Tech Diet.

To answer that question, I'd need a crystal ball.

Or at the very least the Magic 8 Ball that sits on my office coffee table and baffles most kids who ask me how to turn on the touch screen. That's a pretty appropriate reminder of how far technology has come.

I'm willing to bet you had a Magic 8 Ball as a child. Cast yourself back. Would that same child have the vision to predict how technology would be in 2019? Doubtful.

I've danced around the question long enough.

Here are the three main technology advancements that I feel have the potential to change this landscape and that don't appear to be far off mainstream use.

1. Wi-Fi on tap

Many countries have started building free public
Wi-Fi hotspots. In Australia, we're rolling out the
National Broadband Network.

I can still recall the first time I accessed an internet
connection without physically plugging in a device.
It was mind-blowing. And yet, that early connection was
primitive in its speed and the limited distance you had to
be from the router before you were booted off.

**I assume over the next decade Wi-Fi will become
more freely available in public, and be faster
and cheaper to connect.** Many believe this will be a
convenient and productive step for humankind.

**Any parent who reads this book will understand
it could throw up a whole host of challenges in
managing your child's Tech Diet.**

2. Augmented reality

I'm led to believe we're not far off mass production of
augmented reality (AR) technology in smartphones.

Think of a 3D camera that allows you to gauge depth
perception from the real world and replicate that on your
screen. Think of the hit mobile game Pokémon Go but
with 3D graphics while you play.

Great, right? Well, I'm not so sure.

Think about how that could be used by game developers to make games a more immersive experience that, in turn, will be even more difficult for some kids to turn off. Not great, right?!

3. Virtual reality

Around 2011, I remember when a mate had just spent a small fortune on a brand new, cutting-edge 3D TV. He swore it was going to take over the world – but something was lost as we all sat around the screen with those stupid glasses on.

If you're not familiar, **virtual reality (VR) comes in the form of a headset you wear and throws you deep into the experience.** Much more sophisticated and immersive for the user than my mate's 3D TV.

I think the jury is still out on this one. It's already on the market but doesn't appear to have taken off so far.

Perhaps it's the limited games that are compatible?
Perhaps they're too expensive?
Or need some fine tuning? Time will tell.

My philosophy

I suppose this is a conclusion of sorts. But writing a section titled 'Conclusion' didn't sit well with me.

Perhaps that's because so many things in the world of Internet and Gaming Addiction don't have a nice, perfect, neat answer.

Perhaps it's because technology changes so rapidly that I'm constantly having to update the advice I give parents to ensure the strategies will have an impact.

I don't feel that the Tech Diet and the Unplugged Steps are something parents implement in their family and then claim 'victory' at one point in time.

You'll constantly need to monitor your children's Tech Diet and plug the gaps when they open.

I hope this book has provided you with practical strategies you can implement at home to help your children find a healthy balance with technology.

I would be stoked if just some parents clicked with the ideology or philosophy that underpins my suggestions.

If I had to sum it up, my philosophy is that gaming, technology and the internet in general are awesome in so many ways.

But we need to make sure we guide our children to enjoy them at levels that are not going to impact their development from little humans to amazing, bigger humans.

If you resonate with that kind of philosophy, I encourage you to keep troubleshooting.

In a few years' time when the examples I've given are laughably out-dated, the philosophy will remain. It's a matter of you adjusting the philosophy to the new reality and troubleshooting.

Whatever the popular social media platform is at the time, the viral game that's taken over the world or the advancing technology that we only dreamed of in a sci-fi film, **find ways to implement healthy boundaries and ensure your kids live balanced lives.**

If you're more focused on the here and now, I'll leave you with some parting advice.

The strategies in this book are not for everyone. Some parents will feel comfortable with all of it; some may only take a few suggestions on board.

But unfortunately, **the Tech Diet is designed as a wraparound plan. That means, the more you deviate, the more likely you are to get frustrated it doesn't work and give up.**

If you're frustrated, ask yourself: are there any steps or key recommendations I watered down that are now undermining the plan as a whole?

Finally, I welcome your feedback, comments and suggestions.

I practice what I preach.
Technology is not the enemy.

> You'll find me on:
>
> \> Instagram and Facebook
>   **@unpluggedpsychologist**
>
> \> Twitter **@unpluggedpsych**
>
> \> And, for you old-school people, on my website
>   **unpluggedpsychologist.com**

However, you won't find me responding on any of these platforms when I should be sleeping or spending time with my family.

Balance.

Good luck, and all the best,
Brad

Endnotes

1   LM Twenge, TE Joiner, ML Rogers & GN Martin,
    'Increases in Depressive Symptoms, Suicide-Related
    Outcomes, and Suicide Rates Among U.S. Adolescents After
    2010 and Links to Increased New Media Screen Time',
    Association for Psychological Science; 6:1, pp. 3–17.

2   J Katsyri, R Hari, N Ravaja & L Nummenmaa, 'The
    Opponent Matters: Elevated fMRI Reward Responses to
    Winning Against a Human Versus a Computer Opponent
    During Interactive Video Game Playing', *Cerebral Cortex*,
    Volume 23, Issue 12, 1 December 2013, pp. 2829–39.

3   D Lawrence, S Johnson, J Hafekost, K Boterhoven De Haan,
    M Sawyer, J Ainley & SR Zubrick, *The Mental Health of
    Children and Adolescents: Report on the Second Australian
    Child and Adolescent Survey of Mental Health and Wellbeing*,
    Department of Health, Canberra, 2015.

4   American Heart Association: https://www.heart.org/
    en/healthy-living/healthy-eating/eat-smart/sugar/sugar-
    recommendation-healthy-kids-and-teens-infographic

5   K Vella, DM Johnson & LM Hides, 'Positively Playful:
    When Videogames Lead to Player Wellbeing', *Gamification
    2013: Proceedings of the First International Conference
    on Gameful Design, Research, and Applications*, 2013,
    pp. 99–102.

References

Yellow Social Media Report 2018, released June 2018:
www.yellow.com.au/social-media-report/

Bartle, R, 'Hearts, clubs, diamonds, spades: Players who
suit MUDs', *Journal of MUD Research*, 1 (1), 1996:
https://www.researchgate.net/publication/247190693_
Hearts_clubs_diamonds_spades_Players_who_suit_MUDs

Katsyri, J, R Hari, N Ravaja & L Nummenmaa, 'The Opponent
Matters: Elevated fMRI Reward Responses to Winning Against
a Human Versus a Computer Opponent During Interactive
Video Game Playing', *Cerebral Cortex*, Volume 23, Issue 12,
1 December 2013, pp. 2829–39: https://www.ncbi.nlm.nih.
gov/pubmed/22952277

Lawrence, D, S Johnson, J Hafekost, K Boterhoven De Haan,
M Sawyer, J Ainley & SR Zubrick, *The Mental Health of Children
and Adolescents: Report on the Second Australian Child and
Adolescent Survey of Mental Health and Wellbeing*, Department
of Health, Canberra, 2015: www.health.gov.au/internet/main/
publishing.nsf/Content/mental-pubs-m-child2

Twenge, JM, TE Joiner, ML Rogers & GN Martin, 'Increases
in Depressive Symptoms, Suicide-Related Outcomes, and
Suicide Rates Among U.S. Adolescents After 2010 and
Links to Increased New Media Screen Time', *Association for
Psychological Science*; 6:1, pp. 3–17: https://journals.sagepub.
com/doi/10.1177/2167702617723376

Vella K, DM Johnson & LM Hides, 'Positively Playful: When
Videogames Lead to Player Wellbeing', *Gamification 2013:
Proceedings of the First International Conference on Gameful
Design, Research, and Applications*, 2013, pp. 99–102:
https://dl.acm.org/citation.cfm?id=2583024

Acknowledgements

I would like to thank Barbara McClenahan, Lara Wallace, Larissa Bricis and the rest of the team at HarperCollins for putting up with a novice author. Your expertise and guidance were both patient and amazing.

Thank you to Philip Tam, Wayne Warburton and Garry Walter for taking time out of your busy schedules to read and provide your thoughts on this book. You are highly respected, both in my humble view and our wider profession.

Most of all, thank you to my publisher, Helen Littleton from HarperCollins. Naive was I on that day you bought me a coffee and pitched me the idea of a parenting book. It was your enthusiasm and vision that gave me the confidence to think on a bigger scale and, hopefully, to reach more parents than I ever could in my clinic. Thank you for sharing the dream to help families in crisis.

Brad Marshall

B.A. Psych; M.HSc. Beh Sci;
Assoc MAPS

Brad is the principal psychologist at Northshore Kidspace, in Chatswood, NSW, and the clinical director of the Internet Addiction Clinic @ Kidspace, established in 2010.

In his clinic, Brad specialises in the treatment of young people experiencing excessive internet use, or Internet Addiction, and related disorders such as Gaming Addiction, and he helps families find a balance between healthy screen time and problematic overuse.

Brad previously held positions at the University of Notre Dame Australia and in various public hospitals, including Royal North Shore Hospital, Bankstown Hospital and Ryde Hospital, working with children and families as part of the Child and Adolescent Mental Health Service.

Under his new project – The Unplugged Psychologist – Brad is a well-respected presenter and guest speaker, providing professional development to teachers and health professionals, and running seminars for parents, school students and teachers. He also runs seminars and workshops in the corporate space, speaking to staff about the benefits of healthy internet use at home and in the family, and how to be productive and balanced when at work.

Brad has been interviewed for his opinion on a range of mental health issues across the media, including providing consultation for ABC TV's *7.30 Report*, Channel Nine's *Today Show* and Seven Network's *Sunday Night*, as well as giving regular commentary and interviews for various newspapers, radio shows and podcasts.